ONE LEAF SHAKING

ෙ

ONE LEAF SHAKING
Collected Later Poems
1977-1990

Robin Skelton

A Porcépic Book

A division of Beach Holme Publishers
Victoria, B.C.

for
Nicholas

my son and my friend
1957-1994

Copyright © 1996 by Robin Skelton

First Edition

This edition published by Beach Holme Publishers, 4252 Commerce Circle, Victoria, B.C., V8Z 4M2 with the assistance of The Canada Council and the B.C. Ministry of Small Business, Tourism and Culture. This is a Porcépic Book.

Cover Painting: Myfanwy Pavelic
Cover Photo: James Tuohy
Production Editor: Antonia Banyard

Canadian Cataloging in Publication Data:

Skelton, Robin, 1925-
       One leaf shaking: collected later poems, 1977-1990

1st ed.
ISBN 0-88878-370-1

         I. Title.

PS8537.K38A17 1996   C811'.54   C96-900099-5
PR9199.3.S537A17 1996

CONTENTS

*Poems marked with an asterisk have not
previously appeared in a book.*

III. Her Journey

IV. West

VII. Localities

VIII. Are You Listening?

IX. Friends and Strangers

XII. Words For Witches

XIII. Vancouver Island Triptych

PREFATORY NOTE

The poems here collected are taken from four books, two chapbooks, and manuscript. The books are *Landmarks* (Sono Nis Press/Oolichan Books, 1979), *Limits* (Porcupine's Quill, 1981), *Distances* (Porcupine's Quill, 1985) and *Openings* (Sono Nis Press, 1988). The chapbooks are *De Nihilo* (Aloysius Press, 1982), and *Words for Witches* (Reference West, 1990). Some poems have been revised and some titles changed. Several dedications have been added in order to place on record my gratitude for help and support; in no instance does a dedication form an essential part of the poem. The only poem to have been revised extensively is The Visitant; it was in desperate need of surgery.

I have arranged the poems thematically as in my earlier *Collected Shorter Poems, 1947-1977* which appeared in a much enlarged new edition from Beach Holme in 1994 with the title *Wrestling the Angel*. This has enabled me first to perceive and then to present groupings and sequences previously broken up between different publications. Seventeen of the poems have not previously appeared in a book; they are marked with an asterisk in the table of contents.

The title of the book is taken from the poem, "Landmarks" which concludes it.

R.S.

THIS PLACE

&

Neither Trick Nor Treat

Come into this house,
whoever you are.

I am waiting here
with my box of words.

You may have this one
and you this.

I am remembering
Hallowe'en

when the callers were children.
You are not children

playing at witches,
devils, ghosts,

but ghosts pretending
to be people;

this is something
I understand,

being myself
no more substantial

than you who have
no door to time

but stand outside
with threat and promise,

waiting for words
that are more than words.

Watching My House Move

Watching my house move
to the weather,
ever so slightly shifting
its usual stance,
ever so gradually altering
beam and shingle,
the rock on which it stands
looms darkly through
the walls as if it were
a scene that shone
through stage gauze, changing
mood and time and place,
and I am standing
looking at a bare
brown hump of rock
skinned casually with moss
and fern-fringed in the crannies
where a crow
alights black from the islands
on which none
have yet set foot
nor any echo stirred
the stillness with a gunshot,
then it fades
away and I walk through
the claw-scratched door
to rooms in which
our histories are books
and our belongings confident no more
than rock and moss and fern
of what they'll come to,
or of where the past
has let them lie.

In the Stillness

Today I am quiet.
I think I am going to rain.

I am hardly breathing
and breath is thick.

Nothing within me stirs.
I have no thought,

only a heavy patience,
a gathering weight

of nothing I can describe
except by waiting,

and the colours of everything
have changed

as, too, the way I see,
the way I move

slowly into the morning.
Time has nearly

ceased or else is endless,
until now

upon this stone, one drop,
one star of light.

Dogwood

The dogwood is in bloom
for the second time,

white radiance in the green
for the second time

since this year began
with songs and bells

and all the time-worn
Scottish affirmations

that no longer mean
too much ; far better

praise the watching dogwood
for its days

of shining that return
a second time,

asserting there is more
than one beginning.

The Stones

Stones on the porch:
I have forgotten
the field, the beach,

the quarry, the island,
the cliff on which
they slept and were found,

as I have forgotten
those friends who return
in sleep to become

familiar as ghosts
to places and times
they have wholly missed,

walking through doors
they cannot have faced
to hold on their knees

children to whom
they are dead as doornails,
withered as tombs,

then dwindling at dawn.
These stones have paled
in the same fashion,

but lie on the porch,
stone by stone,
embodying a beach,

field, quarry, cliff
and island which
I cannot slough off

any more than the friends
that morning has left
unhoused and unmanned.

Leavings

Dead leaves dug out
of the old hedge bottom:
the years we forget

are there always, lodged
in the roots, pressed
black and solid

by the enormous weight
of fall upon fall,
and hidden from light

by all that has grown,
the tangle and thrust,
the grip, strain and claw,

until for some reason
or without reason
we cut back, lay bare

this that has been, that still
we must know we are,

all the seasons and falls,
all the years and the leaves,
all we left in the leaves.

Watchful

I keep my eye
on the mailbox.
It is watching

out for travellers
round the bend
in the road,

leaning a little
towards the
arbutus (shreds

and tatters
peeling from its
polished trunk)

and shuddering
to the wind (this
chill March wind)

but sturdy still
and secretive.
I keep

my eye on it.
It has been known
to cheat,

accept false
messages and
alter bills,

even some days
when I
venture out

indulge a silent
wide impertinent
yawn,

a sly creak of
amusement.
So these days

I keep good watch.
I have to.
Just last week

I had a word from
God and it was
garbled.

From the Kitchen Window
for Mollie Hargreaves

The snow is surprising the house
with a different, stained yard,
a chill unwelcome peace.

The sky is hard and grey
over the stilted trees
and the birds have gone away.

We had expected Spring
to begin this particular day,
but now the year's gone wrong.

Time is grey and white
and everywhere we belong
is drifting out of sight.

The Innocent

In the backyard
by the rubbish heap
there has been an escape.

The skinny boughs
of the Japanese plum
have begun to bloom

and prink a froth
of pink flowers
pretty as lies

of smiling salesmen,
offering a breath
of renewable youth

to the scarred waste
of a wet garden
grim and forlorn

from a hard winter.
It is outfacing
boredom and loss

with a silliness
that makes us stare,
surprised, bewildered.

It can't be Spring.
The thing is previous.
We know it is wrong.

But just how wrong?
The wind is cold,
March ten days old.

First Day of Spring

It is not
Spring which
moves me but

the thought of
Spring which
moves me and

awakening
I stir
to trees

and troubles
of the restless
air

which are no
more than
shadowings of

what will or
may be
brought to pass

the future
bothers me
with love

the future
bothers me
with death

Note on the Economy

The crows are killing
the songbirds here,
this Spring.

Hoarse from their
broken islands,
they descend

on eggs and young
and weaker birds,
their long

beaks gaping wide,
their talons hooked,
their wings

black, beautiful,
bright glossed;
they perch and call

from branch and roof
and post,
avid for life

and strength through
joy: there's talk
of snares and guns

but we can't kill
and they
won't scare away.

In the Garden

The raindrop slowly
sliding down the leaf

is almost the shape of the leaf,
the shape of a tear

moving of itself
in its own grief

which is not the grief of the leaf,
the hurt of the bough,

but pure compassion
at the way the light

it holds has but a moment
before it falls.

Marigolds

Eyes fading now,
I look on marigolds

clustered orange-yellow
by the fence,

hardy and handsome.
In our big allotment

behind the apple trees
of the vicarage garden

I planted marigolds;
they spread like crazy,

hot to the eye,
as was the sun that summer,

the clay soil baked and cracked,
the little pebbles

shiny and hot to fingers,
and my father

grumped about them.
Weeds, he said, *Just weeds,*

but there was no way
we could get them out

short of pick-axes or,
maybe, explosives;

they were there to stay,
and stay they did

as these will stay
as long as I have strength

to keep untidy splendors
in this place

I need for vision
and for learning how

to burn the neat dead answers
from my mind.

Wild Mushrooms
for Brigid

A stonesthrow from my
old home, in the meadow,
there was a dark green
circle in the grass,
a fairy ring, my mother said,
but Father,
pointing to the small round
mushrooms, told me
Mushrooms do it.
You'll always come on
mushrooms in these circles.
For fifty years I've half
believed him, but,
seeing mushrooms now
upon my lawn,
and not a single circle,
can it be
that he was wrong?
Or did he fantasize
a giant mushroom
like a dinner plate
that spun round in the moonlight
hurling spores

like sparks of Catherine Wheels
out in a circle
till it died, exploded
like a puffball
or sank into the earth,
become the centre
of a tale of dancing
meadow spirits
beating out that track?
It was a track,
a definite beaten path,
I had forgotten
till this moment
just how clear it lay
before me there.
You'll seek for other reasons,
and find them too,
as you can always find
a reason if you look,
for there are reasons
everywhere you wish them:
they spring up
immediate as mushrooms,
but they never
hint of dance, or,
forming deep green circles,
celebrate the powers of
the moon.

Wasp Nest
for Alison

The wasps are building
underneath the iron
bracketted lantern
outside the back door,
steadily overlapping
greave on greave
of papery armour
ribbed and whorled as sands

are ribbed and whorled
by the discovering sea
to form a swollen pendulous
globe, the breast
or belly of some ancient
warrior goddess
of a long-lost tribe
whose dreams and fears
were small and shrill
as are these darts of yellow
flicking through the
heavy air of June,
dangerous and delicate,
or the bulging head
of some decapitated
giant, scoured
clean of all feature,
anaconic, blind
as the beliefs it lived by,
yet there's beauty
here, and dignity,
a kind of trust
in ancient frailties
and traditional skills
that we, too, need,
lodged in this brittle world
hung from the molten
iron of the sun.

Grass and Raspberry Canes
for Pat Neal

It's been three years we
have left the grass

alone around the shuddery
raspberry canes

and seen it rise and thicken,
yellow, flatten

under rain and wind,
spill seeds, entangle

stem and leaf and
firm-packed ivory berries

that plump red for birds
and questing children

happy with wilderness,
but those days are over

and it's all torn out,
earth bare and dark,

specked with a little
dried-out ochre stubble

and the canes shake
as they never shook

while held in swathing grass
protected, stifled,

and their fruit is turning
in the summer,

and the drying grass
is mounded tall

as, in my childhood, I
recall the haycocks

in the close-cropped meadow
by the house

I left to tunnel caverns
in the hay

until the horses
rumbled harvest home,

leaving me roofless
to the dizzying skies

and suns of summertime,
not yet aware

of my own turning
and the thickening blood,

nor of earth's darkness
and the waiting birds.

Grass and History

The grass has forgotten
even the name of history,

if it ever knew it,
and we can't tell

what happened here or when,
but something happened

in that something happens
everywhere,

not that it has to be
what probe and spade

and rake and callipers
can find, name, date,

or those wideminded men
that gauge the earth's

enormous changings;
it could be a thing

that was unknown, unseen;
it could be how

a moth lurched from its shell
with crippled wing,

or how a seed contrived
its huge attempt

to alter every harvest
with a wealth

nobody understood
and no-one found,

or even dreamed,
though time precedes our dreams

too often to suppose
that what we shuck

off in the mornings has not
been before

on the actual earth,
here in the grass

maybe or towering over
it or deep

beneath the browns and
yellows of the roots

we haul up for our plantings,
making history

(we maintain) remembering
man creating

harvests, houses, cities,
banners, names

the grass ignores and
on this cliff forgets

even those creatures
crawling from the sea.

With Help From Stein and Stevens

No-one believes
that if I write of a rose
I am writing of a rose
here in the garden.
I am writing, they say,
of the rosy cross,
the petalled rose of the vulva,
of wounds, of love,

but I write of a rose,
its outer petals
a little ragged, its
inner ones stiff and curled,
its spikes of stamens yellow,
its pistils moving
as the blossom moves
in the moving air,

because the rose is a
rose and only a rose,
and a rose is something
that happens in a garden
and gives pleasure to me,
(*It must give pleasure*)
and pleasure is pleasure is pleasure,
needs nothing more.

In the Fall

Today a small one....
Don't you know

that sort of day
when the wind drops

and reddened leaves
hang stiff and grass

19

controls itself
and fork and spade

against the fence
compose a frieze

of wood and iron
fixed as firm

as grief upon
the broken earth,

so that you turn
away from love

and pride and passion,
bend, pick up

a pebble, hold it,
make it warm,

then, awed and fearful,
let it drop?

Locality

Where is what I am.
The heart is local,
pumps to local breath,
is shocked by sudden
deaths of neighbours,
lifts up at the Spring
seen as five snowdrops
five steps from the door.

There's no mystery in it.
It is common
to us all. We are
our homes and neighbours,
and boundaries we cannot

walk are figments
we accept but know
irrelevant,

made by an alien,
sightless rootless people,
who, having little,
made these little laws,
these little killing laws,
these vast pretensions.
Is this the Russian
or the Roman yoke

we heave to? Is it
Bangladesh or Gaul
whose banners flap
above our small hotel,
whose coinage buys our bread,
whose alien gods
are advertised on our
familiar screens?

It matters to us, yet
it does not matter
in the way love matters
or the sound
of children shouting,
traffic passing, birds
clamorous in the cluttered
evening eaves,

and does not alter us.
Here's what we are
and all we know in ways
that earth is known.
Starve us, kill us,
bury us. We remain
this place, this heartbeat,
this ridiculous house.

The Exhumation

Earth in an open skull
the spade has turned includes

a small pebble that shines.
Not mica, not fool's gold,

but an ordinary pebble
in the expected skull,

and, probing further, here
are other stones. This clay

is full of pebbles. Some
are round as marbles, some

angular, some scarred,
some of a sort of blue,

some brown, some black. Take up
these pebbles in your hands.

The usual needs our praise.
Do not forget again.

Everything

Everything is in the light of everything, holy.
But do not expect a catalogue of grace,
trees, leaves, grass, and children suddenly shouting
Hi-Hi, loudly, running in their playground,
for to select is always to leave out something
quiet, unnoticed, like the snail shell lying
under the black and rotten bit of the gatepost,
or the swing of the signature on the paper,
all of a movement. Everything is moving
in its own direction, sure as owls
dipping the blind hedges, the small stone walls,
in the stiff hills where everything keeps house
within the sound of wind, each, any stirring

slowly towards itself, defeat and conquest,
end and beginning meaningless, arrival
only a word to stand for somewhere else
imbued with what we are more than ourselves.
And this we must remember : every thing
is, before everything, holy and astir
with an unfolding plenitude we are
the heirs of and bequeathers to our sons.
Therefore be thankful when you thank ; be sure
when time assures you on the dragging path;
be kind when you are kindred ; do not lend
uncertainties to strangers or take truth
away from anyone, but still be still
in movement and in peace, the language turning
always upon your silence. Look around.
Everything, before everything, is yours
and none an island—no, none, none, not one
but is the others'. We possess ourselves
only so far as others lean to us
and draw us, moving, into their stirred house
as easily as air, only so far
as everything remains itself and sings.

MY TIME

ల

Three Snapshots

1.

This is an early snap,
too early, for the time
to stand alone and smile
at springtime had not come,
nor has it yet arrived.

I look at that small face
and it cannot look back
through what is future time,
nor forward to the past
as, growing old, can I,
seeing the childhood there
inside me waiting for
its moment when the whole
consequence falls away.

This is an early snap
taken before I knew
what I know now and after
what I shall come to learn.
Shut the album up.
It cannot face the light
too long or it will fade
and stain, not having heard
of memory's hidden strength
and that its richest store
is in the leaving off,
is in the letting go.

2.

This is me
in the old hayfield.

I am nine
and haycock tall

in short pants, knee socks,
and a blazer,

beside a cock
I must not climb

in those good clothes;
my smile is strained

for there, as here,
across the field

the hay wain is
already loading.

3.

Here I am on the river.
It was a girl
that took the picture.
I took one of her
a little earlier,
or perhaps later; it
is difficult at this
late date to be sure
of sequence, and,
quite honestly, the place
eludes me also.
Somewhere on a river
is the best that I
can do, and then
aged twenty two or
maybe three. It is
the camera not the memory
that's precise
enough to trip nostalgia
with questions
guileless as the one
I guess I put

and got this photograph
as souvenir,

and somewhere, cracked and
black, the negative.

In Camera
for Marcia

The camera asks
the questions I would not

ask of any object,
much less person–

dipping into the dark
within me, shifting

surface upon surface,
shaping, sliding,

till I have escaped
myself completely,

and become a different
kind of shadow.

In The Old Family Album

Her children round her, she
holds up an open book.
It shows us she can read.

The hooded lens that took
this yellowing picture gave
her face a stubborn look,

self-confident and brave.
This later snapshot stands
her by her childrens' grave.

No book is in her hands.

The Search

The smaller beasts,
familiar with roots
of trees and faults in rock
where softness fills
cup, cleft, and tunnel,
have near-human cries
when terror grips them,
but, when furled and hid
for winter, sleep
deep under roots.
I hunt
my childhood uselessly
through leafless trees.

The Identification

What I have is distance.
I found it first

one Sunday in the
branches of a tree

beside a weedy stream;
I sat up there

eating cold baked beans
straight from the tin,

and got some sense of it.
Much later on

I gathered words to use
about it, rather

clumsy words at first,
but as the years

went on, I got a bit more
subtle, made

adjustments, balances,
although today's

the first time I have
actually said Distance,

looking across the landscape
to where I am.

A Sort of Symbol
for Jan Grove

Though I don't always use this mug
I feel a fondness for it. I
have used it like this hand, this shoulder,
and this leg. It's not become
part of my heart or soul, but it
has usage–not romance or mystery
but closeness, order, custom. I
would like it to outlast my time.

In New Delhi
for Robin Macbean

Today I am very happy.
I walk the Maidan

and know I am twenty.
I know I am holding the trees

firm in my head in the way
that a child holds marbles.

Her name is Bina.
Her sari is green and gold.

And she is within my head.
It is all in my head,

held firm for the possible
future, for the poem

that I am making now,
for the first time feeling

what it is that I feel
as I feel I am twenty

and own the whole of the earth.
I am surprised

not to be older and wiser.
I read the poem

over and see it is written
in thirty-five years.

Change But No Change

Where we are is where
we have always been.

This house is the house
where I was born

three fields length from the sea.
This basement room's

the one beneath the eaves
where I lay still

to twilit birdsong
in the swaying trees,

and this day is the only
day I've known

for all these years and
farther than these years,

for life's perpetual
and its changing shape

no more than changing
movements of a leaf

that cannot fall
unless the winter come.

and that's unthinkable—
an empty space

that can't sense emptiness.
I twist and turn

that fear around but still
can't dream it through;

I have too firm a hold
upon the bough

and, warm within the sun
that is my sun

of Rome, of Egypt, of
piled stones, of caverns,

of, even, housing grass
and cradling rivers,

shape the same names
to the turning wind.

Here Is

Here, upstairs, is the man
hunched in his study.
Downstairs are his women,

a mother, a wife, a daughter.
He's getting on
in years, but the house is older.

He has filled the old house
with books and pictures,
crowded each space.

Now, in his room,
he is at peace
with a thing called home,

and with something other–
you could say custom–
wife, daughter, mother.

The Enigma
for William David Thomas

This man on the bed
is middle aged
with a grey beard.

Upon his wrist
he has a tattoo,
a sort of bracelet

made up of a spread
rose, shells and leaves;
the rose is red

and his eyes are brown,
unfocussed; he
lies all alone

in the dawn-lit room
except for this poem
that stares at him

through his own eyes
and cannot work
out why it sees

the leaves move, smells
the rose, and hears
tides in the shells.

Gimp
for John Newlove

One of my legs is
longer than the other

and one shorter.
I discovered this

only the other day.
For fifty years

I've innocently kept
a kind of balance

without worrying.
Now I use a stick.

a handsome silver-headed
cane, and keep

a wary eye on steps,
uneven pavements,

and, leaning on my cane,
stoop as I stand

in conversation or in
stores. I wait

longer for crossing lights,
decide more slowly

upon route and distance.
Fifty years

it's taken but at last
I understand

we are what we don't know
when most we are.

A Little Time
for Alison

I have fifteen minutes
before I trudge

in warm and steady rain
along scarred roads

between white houses
and leaf-heavy trees

for no great purpose
unless you believe

that there is greatness
in the gentle words

of man and daughter
at a café table

sharing food and just
a little dry

white wine as sharp and
chill as their lost childhoods.

Then
for Sylvia

It seems like yesterday;
though years have stiffened
bone and muscle,
greyed the thinning hair,
robbed us of earlier
pleasures and illusions,
and brought us sometimes
almost to our knees,

it seems so near still,
perhaps out of reach
but only, surely,
for a little time,
and time's a little thing,
its yesterday
no farther from today
than is tomorrow.

A Good Question

What have I done?
Like wind-pains in the gut
it rumbles through me
and I can't let out
one word of consequence.
What have I done?
Galileo looking at the moon,
Gutenburg at Exodus Twenty Two,
God at Eden:
if they'd thought it through
would they, or could they
have gone on? I guess
Ollie always blamed
Stan for the mess
as Innocent the witches,
Rohm the jews;
abuse is all too often
self-abuse,

an insecurity become secure.
What have I done?
I wish I could be sure,
but, looking back, I'm baffled.
Somewhere there
I must have made one statement,
had one thought
of consequence that changed
one life one jot.
Or perhaps not. What have I
done? This hurts.
Schwitters assembled rubbish
into Mertz
and Picasso built a god
from waste.
What I have done could be
defiled, defaced,
and broken up to make
eventual Art.
It eases me to think it.
I've no part
in that, at least.
I hardly did a thing
except give someone
somewhere to begin,
but even that, I guess,
is something done
and brings its consequence.
Could I be one
that set the scene for
angst, destruction, pain?
Or will I be the man
who set in train
new Heaven and new Earth?
What can I say?
Stan got me in an awful mess today.

Back Again

Themes of return obsess me.
I've come back
so often that the half smile,
puzzled stare,
and cautious recognition
are become
the way for me to recognize myself
as being what I am,
a revenant
only a little changed
by changing times.

Surprise is muted now.
You're back again!
Lost weight! How have you been?
They don't ask where
which may be just as well.
How could I answer?
Paphlagonia? Paramnesia? Hell?
I guess I'd tell them
Just the usual places,
nowhere different,
as if they knew,
as I do not,
those fly-specks on the map,
the black lines and the blue,
the stains and names.

Yet maybe I should try
to spell it out,
like answering the perfunctory
How are you?
with details of disorder,
loss of breath,
and muscle stiffening,
tell them I have been
a different man;
I have to say a man
because it's hard to think
myself a thing

and 'thing's the wrong word anyway.
Let's say
I've been a different thought
a different time

and wait for questions
that won't come, or if
they do will be
unanswerable. I
don't speak this language
when I speak of that.
I do not know what language
I should speak.
Maybe there is none.
I was kept quite busy.
There was always everything to do.
I tell you, it is real good
to be back.
That at least's an accurate
obvious lie

which they may get, or not.
Who cares? I think
sometimes there is no future
in renewal,
as there is no past;
it is all here,
as I am here,
my elsewhere in my eyes,
my hands, my tongue,
the blinding of the light.
I wipe my glasses
and accept a drink
in comradeship,
as if we were all comrades,
as if they had not been
away themselves.

Heritage

With a kind of cough
and a cloud of dust,
(brown snuff of seventy
patient years),
the front of the old hotel
is ripped away;
stacked boxes papered red
and blue and green
and flaked with blistered
paint remain for less
than half an hour,
then everything is gone
but the crook-limbed
garry oak, the fir,
the monkey-puzzle,
and the huddled laurel.

The glass (late art nouveau)
was taken out,
and the porcelain tiles
sold to a dealer
down on Johnson Street,
but the new apartments
will be labelled Heritage
in gold,
and occupied in part
by ladies who
were born around the year
the place was built.

Heritage is a thing
we understand
only when we are losing it
like marriage;
it is what we know
we cannot keep
faith with save by sad
nostalgic acts
of fantasy, recalling
in a shred

of handkerchief,
a faded photograph,
events to which they never
did belong,
and, anyway, whose values
we distrust.

Such is our need and
custom. I myself
have kept my father's
battered old tin hat
and his bandolier,
his ribboned medals.
Someday they'll go—
maybe when I am dead,
or perhaps, some weekend,
wearying of history,
I'll clean house, take them
down to Johnson Street,
or put them up for auction
as collectibles.

Or will my children
call them Heritage?
My mother taps her way
around the house
remembering only that she
should remember,
peering, wondering who,
and what, and where,
much as I do,
lumbering through these rooms,
picking up old books,
collectors' items,
discovered in an
after-luncheon daze
of Beaujolais some place
in Johnson Street
where they'll end up again.
Ambition dreams
of permanence in what we

find to love,
and choices, when they're made,
are planned as final.
That patch of torn blue paper
in the rubble
was surely once well-chosen,
in good taste,
expensive, even envied,
as am I
envied, they tell me,
gossipy with drink
in the beer parlour
just off Johnson Street,

for this old stately house
in which I write,
but it won't stand for ever;
when it's gone
will its replacement be
called Heritage?
And my replacement—
what will they call that?
I know myself the more
the more I age
and begin to lose
what I must lose—
taste, hearing, sight, and,
gradually, mind.
I envy those that pull
the houses down
for they at least leave nothing
to hang onto,
no weight upon their backs
of fear and loss,
no guilt, no desperate memories;
they renew
earth's innocence, and yet
I guess their houses,
too, hold photographs,
those quiet ghosts
that stare out with their

half-remembered eyes
at what they've left us
as our heritage.

Sixty

I take it easy here,
as who does not?
It is the place for it
and I have come
to understand that I
must take my place
among the small
contentments, comprehend
the gentler, subtler
messages of time
that each succeeding day
persuade my ear
a little more distinctly
in the way
that long discarded
languages grow clear
with casual daily use.
Once, I am sure,
I was word perfect
but I don't know when
unless it was–
but you would think me odd
were I to hint at that,
so I'll suppose
it only is the mind,
the aging mind,
that thinks it knows
the roads on which it goes.

Emergence

Everyone tells me these days
that I'm famous.

Squeezing from its cocoon
with crumpled wing,

the ermine moth lies still
upon the stone,

waiting for strength to come
down from the sun

and spread out its black-speckled
satin wings

for some new purpose,
fearing, as do I,

this new, this unpredictable
existence

in an air I have not
learned to breathe

as yet and do not trust.
I'd learned to hide,

but can't hide now.
I'm right out in the open,

and for the small span left
must try to fly.

In Age

In age is novelty;
we have not been here before,

have never come as close
to the smile of death

or as far from the bitter
frown of birth,

have not felt so sharply
the thrust of bone,

the yielding tug of muscle,
the weight of flesh,

have not remembered so much,
so much forgotten;

it is all new, all different,
difference moving

slowly through every part of it,
altering, shifting,

changing the sharpness of taste,
the clearness of sound.

the brilliance of colour,
the nature of pattern,

bringing a different mystery.
What shall we do

when we are wholly different?
What shall we do,

if we do anything?
Or will the nothing

that we must come to inhabit
be all in all

and more than the all we have known,
the slow mind wandering

over the profit and loss,
confused by freedom?

The Endeavour

However hard I rub
I can't rub out
that sly face in the mirror.
It won't go,
not even bits of it,
an ear-lobe say,
or that chunk of hair.
Each day I try
a little harder but
don't get too far.
I've damaged it a bit
beneath the eyes,
flattened and smeared the nose,
and wiped some colour
off the cheeks and hair
but that's not much
to make a song about.
I have a dream
that one day I will find
it simply gone,
completely vanished,
and the space it took
filled in with good clear
details of the room
it's got for background;
well, a man can dream,
and if he works hard
for that dream he may
find it come true,
as mine must, for I labour

all the time; I know it's
taking years,
but one day soon I'll have him
polished off.

Prestigitation

The best tricks are the
easy ones. I turn

from summer into
autumn like a leaf

that's known this all
its life, or like the sun

that shifts its track so
slily you can't say

quite when it happened
though you watched it happen.

The next trick's easier still,
so don't applaud.

HER JOURNEY

ജ

All of Us There Once

I look back
at the small house.
One window is dark.

I am asleep.
Under the eaves
my room is its shape

of stillness and I
in the humped bed
going away

over the fields
and the black hedges
to somewhere old

unknown and good
as are good stories
of warmth and God.

It is not late.
The moon is thin
with beginning night.

My young mother
is hearing the wireless
beside my father.

You know the way.
It cannot be called
a personal journey.

Grimm

In those days
we listened
to all the stories.

Everyone heard
each story
word by word.

We liked the rise
and slow fall
of the voice.

We liked the sound
of pages
under the hand.

It was good
to hear of the dark
terrible wood

and good to hear
of the gold
and the golden hair.

In those days
we hastened
on all the journeys,

hurrying through
this forest
we have come to.

The Concealment

She said *Don't tell your
father!* I'd have asked
what was to tell but
knew it pointless, so
I looked discreet

as schoolboys know to. I'd
not heard of incest,
only gathered something
terrible had happened
with a lad
I'd always liked for
playing crazy games
I mustn't ever share
with him again
because of it,
and *It would Bother him!*
she added, thin-lipped.
Bothering my father
was something I must never
do for fear
of something awful happening–
God knows what–
but God, of course, knew
everything, unless
(I dimly felt) I kept it
from my mother,
as I tried to keep
that dangerous moment
in the orchard when
I had to drop
my spoils and run like
blazes. She found out,
as God, of course, did too,
and then my father
who saw the scare in me
and told me off
without intensity,
quite unlike God
who warned me feverishly
Don't let a girl
get you alone with her.
Something could happen
and you would regret it
all your life,
this being apropos
of our young curate,

who, she said, had been
caught by a girl
and was very silly.
This was worse,
much worse than even
Bothering my father,
impenetrable, frightening.
I nodded,
and thought of him and her
out on the dunes
alone together, then a
sudden trap
that snapped fast, ending
all his hopes for ever,
all his plans and dreams,
and yet the girl
was just as warm and pretty
as her younger
sister whom God saw me with.
You didn't
kiss her, did you? hissed
my mother and
I hadn't even thought of it.
You mustn't,
you know that! she told me,
and I knew
that she and God,
foreseeing shame and ruin,
were terrified for me
as for themselves
obliged to think how not
to Bother father.

The Short Cut

I took the short cut
each afternoon
when they turned us out

of the small warm pub
into October wet
and the hesitant wind,

53

tramping hazily through
the beech-tunnelled wood,
the branches aglow

with early fall fires,
the track black with mud
and packed-down leaves,

along the broad stretch
of stockbrokers' tudor
and through the torn hedge,

arriving around three
at my sick mother's bed.
She seemed glad to see me.

Smelling of beer and a bit
out of breath and astray
I would clumsily sit

for a tortuous chat
about cousins and aunts;
I could get through that

with the three strong pints
inside me blurring
the hour's intense

familiar tedium;
I had found the short cut
to kindness and calm,

and the whole ward told
her I was a good son.
She was acrid and old

with sharp-eyed refusals,
demands and complaints.
I shouldered it all,

heroic with ale
and fresh from the stint
through the tunnelled trees

blazing their fall
and the black rotting leaves
and the dank wood smell

that was age and decay
and strength to pull
through the difficult day

for a hastening Spring.
I went back the long way.
She was not yet dying.

Blackberrying

Here at the back
the berries are thick.
I reach out, hook

her stick round a briar
to haul it nearer.
This I remember.

It does not fade;
she is there, vivid
with hunter's pride,

straining and stretching
this stick to snatch
at what's out of reach,

birdlike, eager,
her heart a flutter
at such dark splendour;

in the grass at her heel
is the scratched enamel
can she will spill

sometime for sure,
her shamefaced laughter
brightening the air

before she kneels
in the grass, refills
it, suddenly small

to the wide blue sky.
I call it a day,
the berries piled high

in my plastic container,
my slow back sore.
I will show them her,

say Look what I got!
She will gape for a minute
and then forget

the why and the where.
I'll boast There are
good berries round here,

and, birdlike again,
she will gaze, brighten,
whatever I mean.

Triptych

1.

My deaf and peering mother
crazy with age
mumbles her supper.

She knows I am not
her growing son.
I'm too old for that.

When she is gone
he'll be left helpless.
She wants to go home.

Her home is with us?
We are talking nonsense.
She is angry at lies.

She hangs onto the handle
of the back door
clutching her bundle,

a crumpled letter, a crust
in a folded napkin.
It is England or bust.

2.

My bent blind mother
deafened by time
hunches her walker.

She means to get
to the front room chair.
There she will sit

without a word.
She has managed it
although it was hard.

Is there anything more?
What would she like?
She does not answer.

It is enough
to have made no mistake.
She has altered life.

3.

My white-haired mother
clutching her blanket
is crying out,

O help me God.
She has lost her wits
remembering the dead

who cannot come
and the sisters she had.
She is lost, alone.

It is two in the morning.
Where is her son?
Will he be coming?

I say I am here.
Her arms are thin.
What else must she bear?

The pillow is soft.
There is nothing to fear
and some time left.

In the Ninety Second Year
of Her Age

We are no longer
family. We are

one that goes shopping,
one she can't disturb,

a teenage girl she often
sees around,

and a cat that's
bothersome, but then

there are the Others
that we know as They

who tell her that she
mustn't, tell her not

to eat this, drink this,
do this, tell her They

will come for her one day;
she is imprisoned,

where she doesn't know,
but she's imprisoned

just like us, though she
is unlike us

in understanding there's
no understanding

this, or us, or what
or who we are.

House Tour

This is the room I died in.
They thought it a pleasant room,
but the windows were always too bright
for the grey fog in my eyes.
I had to keep closing the shutters
against the sun and, too,
against the bothersome faces
of young girls looking in.

They none of them saw the girls,
Lily, Sarah, Jane,
and sometimes Grace. It wasn't
kind of them to intrude
again like that. I wanted

almost to quite forget,
or remember in my own way.
My own way was the way

I'd lived for the longest time,
and who could expect me to change?
This is the kitchen. I used
to put the dishes away
when the dishwasher had finished,
but I got it wrong
too often and had to stop.
It's hard to stop like that.

Along here is the hall.
I walked here near the end
with a stupid sort of frame.
They fretted that I might fall.
Sometimes I did. But I
had been falling for thirty years.
It wasn't any different
except that I couldn't get up.

And now the front room. That
is where he would always sit,
the man who wasn't my son
but spoke as if he was,
and may have been sometimes
in his more gentle voice.
I think it made him cross
to see the bitter end

I only know one more room.
I didn't go upstairs.
No, don't go in. It isn't
decent to show it off.
There was where I had
to come to terms with things
I'd rather not discuss.
They took away the lock.

I think that's about all,
except for the little place
between the inner door
and the door that leads outside.
I struggled a good bit here.
I wanted to get on home.
They said it was far away,
as if I didn't know that!

It was very far away
and they were always near.
I never liked people near;
I kept myself to myself
all the years. I taught
my son to think like that.
Paddle your own canoe
is what his father sang,

and I was paddling my own
canoe in a kind of way,
trying to do it at least.
Independent all
of us girls were at home.
Did I tell you about home?
I'm not sure where it was,
but it was never here,

never, never, never.
Now it is time to rest.
I used to rest a lot.
I couldn't read or hear
most of what went on.
You can go away.
I don't want any dinner,
and I won't go to bed.

WEST

&

Nescience

It was not I who dreamed
these random islands

slanting forest darkness
to the sea.

these broken headlands and
these heaving waves,

nor I who spat out ravens
on the sky;

it was not I who dreamed
but these that dreamed

my footfall and the hour
in which I come

to answer them,
my face a carven mask,

my step an echo
in the painted room.

In the Gulf

There is a great stone head
here on the island.

None on the island
sees it as a head

but as a boulder under
rain-soaked trees

where the tide rides high
in winter storms

and at the surge of Spring,
so some have scratched

initials on it,
and some other things,

not seeing how the great
blind eyeballs stare,

nor how the mouth is fastened
upon silence.

Last Song

Reaching into
a crack in the rock.
to grab the devilfish,
his wrist
was trapped fast
by a great oyster;
none of his kin
could get it out.

Nothing would pry him
loose; no rock
could chip the lip
of the thick shell,
and the tide was rising.
The Spirits of Tide,
he sang to his people,
they are coming!

Look to yourselves!
Bent over, head
bent over, face
turned from the water,
neck straining,
Look to yourselves!
Forced to retreat,
they stood waiting,

listening, learning,
as the sea
surged over
rock and man
and the last of
all last songs,
Spirits of Tide,
they are coming, coming.

Raven's Island

A mist of rain
upon the shore
of the empty island
and in the sand,
half buried, ribbed
as an ebbing wave,
white as the moon,
a gaping clam
bubbling sounds
of human voices....
Whah! Come out!
A small head
peers, withdraws.
A gasp of voices....
Whah! Come out!
Whah! Come out!
A second head,
a third, a fourth, till
(*Whah! Come out!*)
nine heads, then nine
and nine on nine
come out and claim
the island; black
wings flap away.

Indian Graveyard
Vancouver Island
for Rona Murray

The island is a ghost.
Through greys of rain
it humps its black whale;
fathoms of belief
uncountable as years
accept its flank,
and pull the spinning
emptiness of grief
through deep to darker deep;
here, daubed and clad
with every symbolism,
heads roped high
to outstare sunlight
with their flies, the dead
were bound on trees:
years back, men came this way
to look things over,
curious; they found
no human corpses;
not a thought remained
of all the rotting gauds,
but on the ground
and unexplained, dead birds,
whole hosts of birds.

Skin

Skin rose through the water
onto the shell-white shore;

wind blew through the forest
bending the spires of pine.

Skin swayed, swerved, enfolded
the word of the wind.

Skin enclosed the rocks,
gathered up the pool

and moved into the forest,
accepting birds,

the quick eyes and the singing,
accepted mink,

the sharp teeth and the cunning,
accepted bear,

the heaviness, the darkness,
accepted cougar,

the litheness and the dancing,
accepted hawk,

the stoop, the clutch, the power,
accepted beaver,

the hidden hurrying building,
accepted snake,

and then met Raven.
Skin looked up at Raven.

Raven looked down at Skin
and laughed and laughed.

Nootka

Over the west
coast the birds
hover and scream,
the big breakers
hurling them high
to swerve, slide
sideways down
to the shoal, stoop,
dip, strike,
screams echoing
headland to headland,
brown rock
white-splattered,
log-cumbered,
back in the forest
the deer listening,

and those People
Of The Deer,
long dead
but still stirring
dark leaves
with spirit-memory,
still seeing
the white faces,
still hearing
the Yorkshire rasp
of the Chief
with the deep eyes,
first of his race
to tread the island,
meet with the women
of the wind.

Cliff

This is the edge of
breath, a space
where time ends
in a slow fall
down to the sea,
the deep womb
with which all of us
claim kinship,
salt of it sharp
in the warm blood,
pulse of it in
the pump of the heart.
Stand on this edge,
look down, and watch
white birds,
we are told souls
of those lost
at sea whose dreams,
whose wild cries
must haunt and warn
till time ends
all of us, pulls us
out, down
from the last edge
through thin air
once more to drown
through death to birth,
find birth in death,
and claim kin
with tide, with time,
the vast flux
of all that is,
from which we came
to stand on this edge
and face the fall
back to the deep
with changed wings.

Yellowpoint

Nothing happens here but
the slow suck of the deep wave

pulling the round stones free, rolling
them down out of their grey cups

into the gash of the foam, moulding
the round rounder. Nothing happens

but, cup by cup, tides empty cups,
answering the hungers of the moon.

The Watcher
for Theresa Kishkan

From this night mountain
above the lights
you can see the harbour

small as a pool.
I could take a deep breath
and pitch a pebble

away down, over
the town, and break
that glittering mirror,

bring seven years
of desperate luck
on those docks and towers,

but I won't trouble;
it's pleasure enough
to know it possible

and leave them be
as, farther, does
the invisible sea.

Bushed

Someone is lost
in the thick bush
back of the house.

It is not that thick
but the good poem
makes it thicker

to help me out.
I think that someone
must be a child

half-grown and hungry
for old dreams.
I open the door.

Night looks at me
and I look back.
It is not my son

out there in the bush.
It is his father.
The poem is kind.

Susan's Poem

This, your poem, begins here
with light spreading across the sea

and wet stones on the shore shining
up into the brightening sky,

and so I think it must be dawn,
and, though I do not know the place,

I believe I am on an island;
you, I suspect, are somewhere near,

though still unseen, and looking out,
as I, on the impassive sea

to watch—is it a canoe or curragh
coming in? I cannot tell,

not even as it beaches and
a figure steps from it and calls

a name that is neither yours nor mine,
walking off into the forest.

Now he is gone, I see you standing
a little way along the shore

and call out that the poem is yours
whatever it may do or mean.

You shake your head. You say it is
not yours or mine or ours, but is

the poem we neither of us know,
though, sharing ignorance, we share

this watchful space where land and sea
are and are not, where day and night

exist and do not quite exist.
The empty boat lies on the stones.

The poem ends if we enter it;
the poem ends even if we stay.

Poem For Naoko Matsubara
on Seeing her Woodcut,
The Big Tree

Since I am a poet
I must make poems,

but where are the poems,
where are the names and lines?

I think and speak your name.
Here is the poem,

the ancient forest
carved into a dance.

* * *

This vision is
the vision of the tree;

the dream is of its leaves,
its boughs, its roots,

its reaching up and high,
its reaching deep:

the masks it wears
are masks we both have known.

* * *

I can, you say, be recognized
any place–

my unkempt beard, my windblown
tangled hair:

but recognized by whom?
And known as what?

I walk invisible
through fields of cloud.

* * *

You laugh at me.
I laugh because you laugh.

Here is the darkness
that we both have known

and both have conquered,
rending it apart

for light, for life;
our laughter swells the grain.

* * *

It is of the blood
yet not the blood.

It is the service
of another god

that is not of the blood
yet is the blood,

the tide, the river,
the unending dawn.

* * *

No-one can tell us
trees we both have known,

and nor can we tell anyone:
the fact

is beyond question,
beyond every question.

I name. You name.
We interlink the worlds.

Wood
for Naoko Matsubara

There is nothing that cannot be
wood-spoken,

lettered in wood
and spelled out strong by wood,

the language knurled and gnarled
by years of trees,

the syllables a sway
of leaves and boughs,

the thought a dark thought
dipping through the root

to chills of water
hidden deep within

the fundamen, the dream
a shining dream

shaking its leaf to sky
and sky on sky.

There is nothing that cannot
be wood music,

nothing, nothing, nothing;
smoothed and carved

and blessed and healed,
wood builds us, holds us, names us,

guards us, keeps us,
leads us through the doors.

Hemlock

My beauty is the beauty of the axe
that swings down into me its flashing blade,

the servant of the light by which I grow,
its haft the very substance of the term

that it completes in bringing to my birth
its age-old meaning, suddenly the shock

of emptiness, the light, the spreading sky.

The Birch

I bent to the will
of his swinging;
I bent down

far to the ground
for his gripping;
I bent down

from air to earth
for his leaping,
for his breathless

laughter, his guess
at the heavens,
and bent down

under and over
the weight of his youth
to let him

once and forever
reach farther
than his grasp

and higher than
his wishes;
I bent down

in reverence
remembering
the weight of snow.

The Woods

I.

I came to the
edge of the woods and the
woods were there

so certainly and so
breathless with the
moist

decays and rains of
love and death I
nearly

wept as a
man weeps close at
last with his woman

after the exile
day at the
edge of the woods

where night is dark
dawn slow
and the path endless.

II.

The loud house
in the silence
of the pines

that do not change
with seasons
but retain

the dark greens
of the hidden
guiding sea,

the woman
(also heavy
tides of pine),

the forest
(also woman),

hide the stars.

Into The Forest

There are many ways
into the forest

yet the nearest way
is not the way

men mostly go,
brown-shod, red-capped, in autumn,

trampling the wet mat
of the fallen leaves,

but through the moment
in between the moment

when the dewdrop shakes
and when it falls

the terrifying beauty
of a space

in which minutely
memory and terror

meet and are an end
and a beginning,

the glimpsed eye of the deer
through ageless trees.

Above

Sometimes in the bush
the sky is personal,

a purely singular
and private space

as innocent as the
stillness after passion

has exhausted everything
but love

and given love the freedom
of the stillness

in which, mindlessly,
to wander back

to the first glimpse
of the first personal world,

the high bright sun,
the far and singing sky.

The Letter
for Tony Connor

I would have written before
this, but I found out
there were no words to tell
you what the words must mean,

and I was left with small
stones and with white shells
and driftwood, waterlogged,
under madrona boughs,

and I was left with blue
sky and with hunched trees,
gnarled and angular oaks
beside the restless bay,

and nothing else. I would
have written before this,
but there was darkness too;
how could I write of that

without betraying more
of this place than this place
knows or cares to know?
How could I spell it out?

I pick shells on the shore.
The darkness has its place.
The poems are only poems.
I write because I write.

OPENINGS

∞

Invocation

Fanged ship-splitter
woman of rains,
give me the power
again to send

song through the thick
black of the trees,
not to reveal
what enters me

as bear, as thunderbird,
as crow,
as blackfish, raven,
salmon, mink,

nor to explain
what mask I wear–
but to recall me
to the ring

of fire and bring
the only words
that have the strength
to face the trees,

to pierce the thunder
of the waves,
woman of words,
tide builder.

Sum

*For I have been ere now a boy and a girl, a bush and a
bird and a dumb fish in the sea.*
                              –Empedokles of Akragas

What I was once, I was.
What I am now

84

I do not know. I have been
bird, bush, fish,

have known air earth and water,
have survived

the wrinklings of the earth,
the heaves of seas,

the cloud-split and the
gale, and I have come

to this that does not know
what it has known,

but has the skill to
dream it, slip through dream

to rediscover blurred
uncertain things,

the thrust of air, the
wetness at the root,

the green of darkness,
the entrancement both

of being and observing
boy, girl, bush,

bird, fish, and dreamer
in one moving whole

that does not move
away from or towards

but through the life of things
to say *I am*

at waking, and, at waking,
Who am I?

turning upon the pillow,

lost and endless.

Sleeper

Tomorrow I'll sleep in this bed;
for the very first time

I will trouble this pillow
and rumple this sheet

that itches under my chin
as I write these words

and, lying back, for the first
time see this ceiling

that now is so familiar.
Tomorrow I'll find

I am looking ahead to this moment,
wondering when,

if ever, it will come,
if ever tell me

what I would tell myself
if I were older,

if I were not a stranger
to sleeping here.

Our Place and Theirs

Somewhere we are
ghosts, our features
blurring air
between window and door,

this warmth we feel

and breathe reversed
by time's mirror
into a chill,

these words a murmur.
Those who glimpse
us poised within
the usual room

cry out in fear,
call in the priest,
the wise old woman
unaware

that somewhere they
are also ghosts
blurring air
between window and door.

The Doorways

I could not get into your dream.
You locked me out.

There was a great red door,
the red of cedar,

carved with the masks of wolves
and the fins of whales

and the spread claws of birds,
and dawn was coming

over the island mountains;
I could not get

into your dream: my mouth
was fastened shut

with sinew thread; my hands

were bound by creepers,

and my ankles hobbled.
I turned away

down to the shore and
stumbled into the water,

and you rose through the water
into my dream.

The Sharing

I think you are asleep.
I am your dream.

Tell me the pathway
that I have to go.

I walk a narrow track
between tall rocks

beside a silver river
far below.

And you are not asleep:
I feel you wake.

The rocks, the river,
and the trees are gone,

and all I hear is your
heart pound.
O sleep,

sleep now. I will be
present at the dawn.

O Lazarus

Lazarus, old companion,
give me your hand
It's lonely here,
the emptiness more vast
than any darkness.
I forget my name
sometimes and wander,
wondering whom they call

into these forests
and along these trails
until trails end
where silence is more loud
than even echoes
of the driving sea
that trouble me
both sleeping and awake
with cumbering vocables
of rock and storm
that, black as bibles,
thunder of a god
I cannot face;
here in the green-lit shade
of throbbing stillness.
It is not that god
I fear but my own pulse-beat
joining in
the myriad pulse-beats
of the gathering trees
that watch in silence
as I ease my pack
and squat upon a rock
as old as time
that, suddenly, I see
wears on one flank
half-hid by moss
the channels of a glyph,
a figure neither

beast nor man, yet both,
asking acceptance.
I no longer ask.

I know that I no longer
can belong
to any tribe or family
or creed.
Lazarus, my old outcast,
tell me now
your story of escape,
your tale of seas
that opened under you,
of rocks that moved
aside like shadows
when the sudden light
alters direction
at the shouts of guards.
We have no guards now.
We walk on alone

into these forests,
and I need you here.
This glyph is terror
and a kind of love.
I touch it and the trees
begin to move
around me in a slow
and burdened dance,
their movement like the sea.
I hear the sea
once more within
the sussurrus of leaves,
and know the tide is
everywhere I move
and every tide is spelling out
that god
whose truth and mercy
hallow and destroy
us all with freedom,
letting loose the light
upon us, and the blindness

in the light,
and if we have escaped him,
you and I,
at least so far,
it is because he wills,
as does this glyph,
another darker claim
upon our journey
than his finite plan
for other creatures
(if such creatures be)
that can at last
lie down between the trees
or in the darkness
underneath the waves
content to be the smallness
of themselves.

Or so I say now,
pulling back the moss,
searching the stone
with palp and broken nail,
to come to terms
at once with near and far,
with man and beast and bird
and fish and tree
and history
and darkened memory.
O Lazarus, old companion,
will we die
ever again, or,
should we die, return
to this–this sea, this forest,
and this stone?
O Lazarus, is Lazarus my name?
Am I forbidden death
as is the world?

Waiting

Why do you leave me alone?
I am scattered without you,

white broken shells on the shore,
a torn branch lying

angular upon rocks
a shred of cloth

caught on a twig of madrona,
a broken leaf,

and have no voice or footstep,
no dream or shadow.

Have you not thought of a name
in which you can come,

a shape, a face, a form?
The wind blows through me,

and the waves beyond the bay
flash white

as more madrona leaves,
tugged from their shadows'

crowded whisperings, spin
along the shore

and the sky grows leaden.
Is it in

the storm that you will come,
or, after storm,

the slow and stealing peace,
the spreading light?

I wait. I am scattered without you,
random. Can it

be that this is how, at last,
you come?

Outside

It is outside it.
Though you suppose
the shrine, the lamp,
the time-worn stones
the heart of the matter,
they are thin
as paper upon
a paper screen,

and yet no shadows,
(coloured shadows
cast by shapes
that block the light)
nor even echoes,
(altering shifts
and swerves of cadence
from one Voice);

they simply are
the outside, as
this is the outside,
print and speech
telling us nothing
but that we
speak from the outside,
live outside.

The Rule
for Ludwig Zeller

There is a rule
applicable to children–

which we should not
at any time forget.

Thus, when a bull's
discovered in the garden

or a unicorn
ascends the stairs,

we must not call the
wide-eyed tale a lie

or even speak about
imagination,

but accept realities;
we, too,

see what we do not see
and cannot know.

In the Cave

Today I made a sound
and no sound came back.

I was a darkness speaking
into the dark,

a depth expecting
profundity of depth,

a journey wondering
about the journey.

And I made another
different sound;

it was a quite small sound,
a questioning sound

that nothing answered.
I heard nothing answer.

There is nothing more
intense than nothing

at these times. I will not
tempt these times.

I will be silent now.
Now I will listen.

Stone-Talk

Put your hand on
stone and listen, not

with your ear or your
mind but with your fingers,

to the changing
syllables that spell

out sentences you have not
met before

save in the scratch of
bark upon the hand,

the rasp of grass between
the naked toes,

and listen (through your
fingers, through the throb

of pulse, the hiss of
skin) to all the words

that are beyond the words
we think we know

and are the knowledge that
we think to words.

Knowledge

Knowledge does not arrive
by studied labour;

though you hunch year on
year above your books

and Bachelor, Master, Doctor
of each science,

labour farther to
enlarge your mind,

you cannot come to
knowledge; that eludes

deliberate effort as
does ecstasy,

and must happen
suddenly, your startled

understanding falling
to its knees.

The Simple

Make it simple
I told myself.

But it was simple.
I didn't need

to make it so
but to unmake,

let go the leaves
and see the sky.

The Secret

I would like to say
the secret is old,

but it is young,
perpetually newborn.

I would like to call it
a holy secret

but that's absurd
for everything is holy.

I would like to describe it
as wise and learned

but only the shadow of it
is found in books.

I would like to tell you
the secret, but

only those who know it
can ever be told.

The Other Way

The only thing we remember
is the past.

Consider this: the past
is all we have

to think about and with,
to shape us so

that we know that we are
(we say) ourselves

and nothing other.
Yet there is that other

we are not quite yet,
or maybe are,

if we could only trespass,
climb the fence

into the other place
and not look back

but forward, think
in terms of a becoming

unattached to memory,
think of what

we say is *unpredictable*,
call *unknown*.

and grow familiar with it,
as we've grown

familiar with these dead
that fill our houses.

The Painting

You have seen it,
the lady with the dragon,

she leading it with a
riband round its neck

down from the cavern
in the great hill mound,

and have presumed some
conquest over evil,

not recognizing
mutual reverence, she

being privy to the
dragon-power

that rocks the towering
menhirs in their beds

above the crossing
waters, and he trusting.

woman-lore, the changes
and the seasons,

both rapt within the
trance of generation.

One Night in February

The pillow is hard.
I pummel it over the darkness

it holds down and think it
soft and deep,

telling my bones to be still,
my heart to be still.

I meet a phrase I know.
It is *Wayland the Smith.*

His unnamed bride is young,
a river daughter

naked yet dressed in water.
It is Spring

here in my head. I turn
the pillow over.

I do not know the story
my memory knows

but try to think it through.
There is iron and water,

an iron ring in the water,
a ring of water

and an April pillow.
I trouble the water

and move the pillow an inch.
It is three o'clock.

The darkness under the pillow
is heaving softly.

My wife has begun to snore.
I am being married

again in Wayland the Smith,
in the river maiden,

in the wide, slow, sweep
of the morning Rhine

between Metz and Coblenz.
This, I remember,

was in July, not April.
I shift the pillow.

Flux

Moving between
continents of sea,
the earth heaves, ripples,
rises, falls,
presents a mountain
that becomes a deep,
shifts in its colouring,
green to gold to bronze,
swells and diminishes,
as the seas remain
changelessly themselves,
responding only
to the steady
tugging of the moon,
the sliding of the wind.
How can one chart
the hills and forests
in their constant change,
how set a course
from valley into valley
when the seasons move
the very earth
one travels as one travels,
and how find
a steady anchorage
in these heaving hills?

There is no settled
anchorage or haven.
As I watch, a house-beam
crumbles, falls,
a tree thrusts rock apart,

a mountain slides
a hundred houses down
into brown clay
and flame chars half a
green-clad county black,
and there's no certainty.
The child we knew
is now a man we do not
care to know,
and he that killed our fathers
calls us friend.
What is identity?
The man I was
walks through these words I write,
his alien eyes
accusing me; the man
I may become
stands in the doorway
mocking what I say.

Prayer Before Birth

I cannot pray for myself
Only just can I bear to ask
for words which are not for me
but for the grinders and yellow tusks
of this creature to crack,
crush, and make paste;
I don't know what he is,
but the tracks where he has passed
smell hot and rank. I do not
pray to the gods but to him,
the malignant judge, the sweltering heart,
the brute reason.

And pray for you,
though not to get you words,
but different blessings
like muscles that are lean and hard,
eyes that are clear, teeth sound,

four fingers and a thumb on each hand,
and only one head.
I ask that you have
strength delicacy and innocence in love
often satisfied on a firm bed,
and a good thirst, a strong hunger,
in the appetite passion, in the mind order.

I ask also the creature to whom these words
are addressed and to whom they fall
that he may remember my devotion, the bared
flagellant back, the hairshirt, the clumsy cowl,
and, leaving my pellets of skin and split bone
on your step,
breathing with breath I gave him,
rear and rip
down all your failures, giving you the intent
lost desperate courage that alone
is worth prayer or defilement.

A Fourteenth Way
of Looking at a Blackbird

One path only is left for us to speak of, namely, that It is.
—Parmenides of Elea

It is a bird upon
the slim-leafed rowan.

Is it a bird? Is it a
rowan? Let

us add that it is I
that speak of this,

that am enquiring what
I see, that it

is in these questions that
the bird and rowan

are, as well as there;
let us prepare

ourselves for thinking
we are and belong

also here, in this,
and that it is

a crooked track we take
who care to look

on any bird on any
sharp-leafed rowan.

Openings

Openings:
The ice widens
darkness between blind mirrors
where I walked that winter, sliding
seven years of breathless life
between hedges;
ice widens
darkness between the crags of light
and mounded whiteness of a North
I must imagine if I dare
to speak of winter, dare to think
of openings in the frozen mind
that must break open into darkness,
opening in the darkness forms
of goat, of bear, of swan, of cross,
of mathematics of the light
that calculate the track of time
and openings in time.
I see
time opening and retreat, recall
there was an opening in the cloud
that showed a sudden country, green
and definite where purple sea

spread wide its cloak till then, a place
unmapped, ephemeral. Clouds closed
and engines rumbled.
We are over
land. This is your Captain speaking.
The local time is now high noon
and elsewhere midnight.

She at midnight,
opening her gifts, *it is*
my birthday now, so can I open?
You may open. *It's a love!*
Truly a love! How did you find it?
opening wide her tired eyes
as if through black and narrow rocks
green-stained by tide and scarred by tide,
holding her breath, expectant, she
had happened on another sea
of limitless irradiance with
a smooth expanse of untrod sand
that only children trust and know
belonging upon every shore
of every proper ocean and
no place for ice.
Ice opens, dark
the widening water, dark the night,
and dark the mirror, bright the stars
through whose far mesh we seek to move
to farther openings.
We call
them 'openings', those gaps that we
must push through in our affluent dream
of progress gathering age and praise
until we face an opening that
we can't avoid but stumble through,
helpless, never having paid
attention to that hidden fault
hair-triggered to bring ruin down,
replace a mountain with a sea,
the lakes with deserts, deserts with
the slow inevitable forests

to be named by others who
are still to come, or who have gone,
for this is not of Earth but Time
and it is Time that is the fault
which opens suddenly into
another opening
and another opening.

A Gathering For Lovers

ॐ

Possibilities

It could be the first time,
couldn't it? All we need

is to know it the first time
and it is the first.

It could be the best of many,
couldn't it?

All we need is to feel it
to be the best

for there to be no question.
It could be

the last time, couldn't it,
the end of need,

the last time at last?
It could be, couldn't it?

Don't Get Me Wrong

I didn't mention it
in the other poem,
(which isn't printed here),
because I'd hate
for you to think I like
your lovely body,
(which I do)
more than your haunting verse,

for I do not (I mean,
prefer your body).
Nevertheless I'd like
to mention that
your loving is as
memorable as your lines,
in case you think
by leaving that theme out

I meant to hint that I
delighted in
your verse more than your bed,
(which I do not),
though verse lasts longer
in a way. I don't
mean you are getting old
or losing shape;

I simply mean the poems
stay on the page
and do not change,
whereas you leave your bed,
remake your face,
transform yourself. I did
not care to mention it
in the other poem

because it could be
misinterpreted,
and poets are good at
misinterpretation;
it's our profession,
as, of course, is love,
which you well know
so I've not mentioned it.

The Hesitation

This, written to my dear, begins
with candid hesitation, for
the space in which the words appear
is ruled by Time's tyrranic law,

and yet we have outdistanced time,
outdistanced even distance in
our unity of love and mind,
so even now as I begin

this written for your eyes I know
there's no beginning and no end,
and, hesitating, must forego
what I would send my dear, my friend.

Time Zones

This pale dawn I
would put my hand in yours,
but you are lunching
under noonday sun.

This mid-day I
would offer you these blossoms,
but you are drawing on
your evening shoes.

This evening I
would touch your cheek, but you
are stepping into night
and do not turn.

A Leaf of Privet

If this leaf
means anything
it does not
mean as words do.
You agree to that?

If these words
mean anything
they do not
mean as kisses do.
Is that agreed?

Now you expect
a third term
in progression.

I will not provide it.
I will say

only that your mouth,
shaped like a leaf,
engrosses me
with its half-
troubled smile.

Palimpsest

It is to be in love with a woman
long held by another man,

her voice, her turning head, her hands'
unthinking gestures, part of him.

It is to know that there are moments
when she smiles that you become

almost the kindred of that man.
It is to know these moments few.

It is to be without the words,
the inner knowledge of the words,

her heart's familiars, moving through
her days of comfort and despair

with an assurance you have lost.
It is to think her memory on

another place, another woman,
footprints bruised into the stone.

The Awakening

Whoever you may be, pretend
that we have never met before
the shock of ancient knowledge felt
between us opens such a door
upon the light that we must shield
our eyes with this absurd pretence
or, dazzled, reel, the shaken heart
disordered by this confluence.

After John Donne

I want to get you where you live,
the clapboard house with straining steps
up to the creaking porch, the small
wallpapered room above the store,
the door anonymous in beige
blank at the far end of the corridor.

And I want to hold you there,
pin you against the mottled wall
or looming slippery fridge, or in
the vinyl of the deep armchair,
and tell you–but what I shall tell
I will not tell you now in case

it should forewarn you; I must be surprise
and you–you must reveal the man I am.

Herself

Time changes in her;
hours contract, expand;
her hands wave centuries aside;
her mouth,
engulfing aeons,
gags upon a minute;
predictions become
histories of truth,

and all theology
a children's rhyme
scratched by a nail
on God's sarcophagus.
She spends a month
of Summer on a smile
and locks up Spring
and Winter in a kiss.

The black and circling hand,
the draining sand,
the altering candle,
the repeating tide,
even the swell and dwindle
of the moon,
the rise and fall of sap
she sets aside

as an irrelevance
she does not need;
with young girl's hands
she paints Egyptian eyes
to stare out from the bed
upon far night
as if the serpent offering
in her thighs

reclaimed the birth
of Always for the world
of everywhere she chooses

to become,
each wanton kiss,
each soundless timeless word,
the universal
spasm of the womb.

When

When she came in from the garden
with the flowers
I started reading Tacitus.
When she put
the roast into the oven
I remembered
my first amorous kiss
behind the workhouse.

Do not thinks that I
describe division,
alienation, all those
anxious words;
I am discussing root and leaf
and flower,
the mingling currents
that create the tides.

The Rover

To go elsewhere is to abstain from movement
                                                    – W.H. Auden

To go elsewhere is to abstain from movement.
Here is the bed within which Helen drowned
necessities of youth. You will not find
an empire older than your frightening pillow.

To seek new loves is to avoid love's history,
its throned intelligence, its heritage,
its towers and pinnacles confronting fall;
the architecture of the heart is age.

To go elsewhere is to exclude from movement
all those feared familiars, to bend
the shaking spreading sheets with ropes of sand,
and yet not find a world more strange than yours

but mere Americas whose differing tribes
are shadows of the restless bedroom floor
upon which lendings fall as travellers' hands
attempt the navigation of despair.

To Robert Graves

'Honest Lover' is
your phrase, not mine.

I find it hard to
think it possible,

such close attention
to details of debt,

such probity regarding
trap and ransom,

and, if honesty
pertains to speech,

what lover's not a
thief and unashamed,

stealing from all and,
from you, 'Honest Lover',

too passionate to heed
ownership or care.

Blue Lake

From lake and trees
I send you strength.

The axe-head stones
nudge ropes of roots,

the chipmunk flaunts
his stripe of tail,

the shag of green moss
humps our bones.

From trees and lake
I send you simple

ecstasies; the
squirrel leaps

as fire leaps
from fallen tree

to fallen tree;
loon-laughter peals.

From wilderness
I send you peace :

woodsmoke at nose,
the hiss and crack

of dead branch burning,
and the huge

blue dragonfly above
red flowers.

Poem Concluding
With an Obvious Falsehood

This is a real man
watching you. Don't think
it is only a poem.
I have abandoned that
absurdity. Don't think
either that it is me.
It is a real man watching
you from across the room.

He has not got a name
quite yet. You can make it up.
He'll answer to it if
you call. It is his name
that you have made, as he
is someone I have made
to be with you–not me,
(I think I told you that),

but real as real can be,
which sounds a bit unreal
because we do not know
what real may yet become,
and yet these words are real
enough for both of us,
and I am real, and you,
and he, across the room,

not speaking yet. You must
decide what he can say.
He'll say what you believe,
(that is his favourite trick),
but mostly he will watch
so I can turn away
from thinking of you there.
I have abandoned that.

The Poem Mistaken

The poem says this
is a poem for you.
I think it lies.

Though you are here
where the poem begins,
brushing your hair

before the glass
in your book-lined room,
it is not your face

it is conjuring up
as the echoing words
move step by step

towards their end
and silence, yet
the poem must pretend

to speak to someone.
It has picked you,
asks you to listen

just long enough
for it to put
pretences off

and here admit
it has nothing to say.
Will you comfort it?

A Walk on Sunday

I walk into the forest
as you walk.

This is not remembered
or foreseen

but happening,
as in different rooms a flower

lets a petal fall
the self-same fashion

in the self-same instant
as a hand

in different centuries
plucks the self-same shape

from time and air.
I tell you that I walk

into the forest
as you walk. The forests

are two different forests
and yet one.

I feel your tread in mine
you mine in yours

before we move into
the separate glades.

She

She was blonde, black-cloaked; her voice revered
the shapes of syllables; her arms were thin,
her green eyes dark with searching out lost selves
across far memories and through truths.
                              I lie
under the desolation of a sky
blue with its miracle and hear the wind
shuffle the leaves and swing the arrow round
upon the slatted mill to eat the storm.
Something is somewhere crying to be born.
I fear it in my heart, but dare not peer
or pull aside the ribs to unhouse light

that might strike passion blind, afraid to find
again Her face, Her voice, Her touch, Her smile.
The great mill arrow shudders in the storm.

Light in the darkness, darkness housing light :
there is a way to turn an image round
until it fits the cavity in faith
and so presents whole armour to the sun.
But if the image is a human thing
it raises mortal needs and will not turn
the easy fashion that the mind demands;
it walks upon the stage and has its words
and perturbations pat; it holds out arms
to pains and children, kissing as it chides,
and, at the curtain, slides between the sheets
to drive or to be driven into hells
I face as I must face Her image now,
bright-tressed, night-cowled, her mouth a pleasant thing,
her green eyes gentle, her discoveries true,
and Memory, like a phantom of the moon
hung white above the waves that pulse and suck
devotions of their servitude, extends
a re-awakening pain. Must I recall
what I am bid recall? Must I ascend
that stair again and meet those dreamless eyes?

What's necessary if not of the soul?
Yet what is of the soul? The wind has dropped.
The looming arrow's still, but it will change.
I turn from love to love as arrows turn
upon their towers beneath this dazzling sky.
To seek Her image is to live in fear
of ecstasy and fear of its despair
and struggle as I struggle, whispering prayers
that what is lost may not be wholly lost
and what recovered kept some little while.

LOCALITIES

ဩ

The Places

Among the many places
I have forgotten
there must be one
that made me linger here
because of some similitude
or difference,
some worn familiar tree,
some warmer shore,

for I remember
every new encounter,
every stranger strange
because not strange,
and within every word
I hear an echo;
even my own face
is my own face

repeated, long known
from another glass
I can't recall,
except that it was there
where I have been.
I know that I have been
there before here, and,
maybe, later, here

will be remembered
when, again, I'm there,
if I should go again,
if I can go
away from anywhere,
leave anywhere.

Looking For It

Somewhere around here
is the very edge,

a lip of cliff above
the broken sea.

It may take time to find;
the bush is thick.

and even though I've
happened here before,

indeed keep coming back
to it, I never

can be sure I'll make
the scene again

and less sure I'll be able
to draw back

when the enormous
vacancy of air

sets me leaning over
that vast whelm

as if poised to plunge,
yet I must pace

out on that lumpy turf
and stare below

to feel the surge that fills
the heart of things

if I am not to end
in a small house

of cramped and bitter stone
with nothing earned.

Checking Out

This morning three
red spots of blood
on the desolate sheet

and five black hairs
on the dented
rumpled pillow;

this morning two
clenched towels
heavy with wet

on the yellow tiles
of the empty
bathroom;

and this morning
something that once
was perfume

stifling the still
drawn curtains of
the room

no-one lives in
anymore,
the key

lying upon the
table, fanged
as lightning.

The Performance

Dozing over my book,
I'm walking

down a smoky street
past shuttered

shabby one-room shops,
flayed doorways,

flaking red brick
smeared with grime,

and iron lamp posts
to a place

of sudden lights,
a rustling crowd

shuddering the dank
rain from umbrellas

and pale raincoats,
waiting for

the clumsy orchestra,
the heavy

thick red curtain
and a play

I haven't seen yet
though I know it

is my own and
one of terror

ending in a sudden
darkness

through which I
must stumble home.

On the Spanish Steps

He took off his shoe
on the Spanish Steps.
There are explanations:
his foot was sore,

he had picked up a nail,
his toes were hungry
for cool air, but
explanations matter
only if it matters
to find cause
and, after that, effect
and link them up.
I'd rather take the
thing itself and hold it
steady, face in mirror,
fly in amber,
for whatever time
it takes to see it
clear and see it whole.
He was quite young,
I'd say round seventeen,
most likely German;
the sock was powder blue
and his hand tanned
with bitten fingernails.
It could be Durer,
Goya, anyone
observing, capturing
the instant, but
it happened to be me,
and I turned away;
I did not need
to see more than I'd seen
of shoe, sock, skin.
Death, too,
takes but a moment.

Roman Holiday
for William David Thomas

Rome. A hot day.
Spitting cherry pits
on the uneven paving
of a street
I've lost the name of—

black fat juicy cherries
from a paper bag.
Footsore. Not limping
yet, but footsore.
It's not in the notebook.
Neither is the young
man in the Forum
with a Tee-shirt
branded Iowa,
nor that flash of terror
half across
the wide white roadway,
and the squeal of cars,

but notebooks that have
everything have nothing
but themselves. They do not
reach or press
for answers. They present
conclusions: *Bought a bag of
cherries, ate them.
Met a student. Almost
knocked down by a
maniac in a Fiat*
leaves out what it was
to say what happened
and would stop me
saying how I saw:
Rome. *A Fiat in the
Forum knocking
down a student spitting
cherry pits.*

After Custer Died
for Diane Keating

After Custer died
I took the subway
down to Yonge and Bloor
to have an Irish
in The Golden Nugget.
It was five,

I think, or maybe
half-past. I drink Irish
in Toronto, in
Seattle bourbon.
You know how it is.
I have to wait
between appointments.
It was afternoon
before my war began,
a single plane
(a Messerschmitt)
alone above the Humber.
That one took some waiting–
fourteen years,
give or take a month.

Still, there at seven
suddenly she was.
I had to tell her
after Lincoln fell
I climbed a tree
and very nearly died
of fright. She says
she suffers too
from vertigo. We laugh
together. She drinks
whisky sours. I can't
explain the joke. It
may have been the times
we live in made the point
or lost the point.
This was after Kennedy
was shot.

A Seat in the Movies

Begin here. The soldier is dying
in rags and blood.

Behind his head the cathedral
is talking mist

to arch and gargoyle and buttress
and grey smeared saints.

Beside him a sodden notebook
ruffles and broods,

and we know that this is the notebook
we are to read,

or look through, seeing his childhood,
his youth, his girl,

his terrible adventures,
his moment of peace

when he decided ...
but what he decided is here,

slumped by the crumbling tombstone,
accepting a drink

from the flask of the comforting woman
whose flawless hair

tells of her inner purity,
though her clothes

clearly allude to her being
some class of whore,

which promises well for the notebook
when we get

past the first page and the names
of the stars, the director,

and the one who thought up those astonishing
special effects

which seem to have made no difference
when everything ends.

Kinship
for John Pass

Kin, Kinship, Kindred....
The look of the words
bothers my head;

that angled beginning,
that whistle-thin
second comer, that n,

a small door, narrow
to hooped shoulders,
give me a shudder

I can't shake off. It's
a stone-hacked hut
the ninth century built

on a dank headland,
a lean shrill child,
and a man with a sword;

it's a scooped cavern
in rotting sandstone
where guns have driven

the sparse survivors
of indian wars;
and it is a house

lit by one candle,
the Cross twisted
to hate on the threshold,

yet these words bring
warmth, safety, things
that haunt our old songs

of the terrible need
for a gift-bearing tide,
a sharing of dread,

and something I can't
put a phrase to yet
that, clenched as a fist,

hate, envy, pain,
lust, cannot distrain–
the last thing we own.

The Last Resort
for Christopher Wiseman

No-one is dancing here,
not even Gene Kelly.

The bandstand has iron green
pillars that glisten in rain.

and behind the rhododendrons
are souvenirs

of undeniable lovers
and undone girls

who are not dancing either,
not tonight

here, or in the Palais
whose lights are out,

and the only music left
is the slow shoed shuffle

of tides invisible over
the lip of the cliff

and the far whine of a car
on a coast road journey,

desolate as my heartbeat
and the band

that surely must have played
here is remembered

only by the stars that
do not dance.

Source

Somewhere back of my days
there is a river

shovelling stones
down sloped of sliding rock,

licking and lashing
the red stems of alder,

turning over and over
its every thought

in a perpetual
solitary passion.

High in the hills it is:
none has been there

for centuries perhaps
or perhaps ever,

yet I know it
back of all my days,

shining, shivering,
rushing steel and silver,

waiting for my star
to lead me on

to see it, feel it
for the first, last time,

and climb up through the trees
into the cavern.

Those Afternoons

Over there is the tavern
I used to wait in.

The leather on the chairs
was cracked and split,

the chrome stained yellow
on the curves, the heavy

big glass ashtrays scratched,
their names rubbed out,

the Schlitz sharp, chilling.
Boarded up for years,

it's found itself new
management. I expect

they'll have replaced the
broken Wurlitzer

and sanded the uneven
heel-stabbed floor,

but I don't want to go in,
not in company;

it had a private meaning.
I sat waiting

there for nothing I could
name, just waiting

hour on hour through slow
dark afternoons

and thinking, as thought blurred,
what poems might do

or say, what I might
say or do if I

discovered, as could happen
if I waited

patiently enough, just
why I waited.

Twice

The first serpent
was green, crushed
by a boot or stone;
dog roses
nodded above it;
hooked briars
writhed and tangled;
I smelt salt
on the sea-wind:
Harmless, harmless
my father said,
and we walked on
to where the sea
with yellow foamy
jaws mouthed
the brown cliff
and ate acres,
spitting stones
back at the slithery
clay, tumbling
wall and hedgerow;
on the cliff,
we watched, marvelled.
The second serpent
was invisible.
We saw
only the papery
silver skin
cast off under
a bush; the desert

withered and wrinkled
round for miles
and she was frightened.
harmless, harmless
I said softly
and we walked on.

Fish Eagles

We counted twelve of them
above the meadow,

great wings silhouetted
on the sky,

swaying upon the wind,
and sliding, gliding

round what seemed a
sacred space of air

they dare not verge upon,
and we supposed

somewhere below that space
that there was something

necessary, some small life
whose cry

held them within the pattern
of that slow

and circling ritual
which would not cease

until death entered.

Prince Edward Island
for Moncrieff Williamson

Snow-firm and flanked by snow, the road
drives forward through the island mist
this February morning and
all substance has become a ghost

half recollected from a dream
whose harsh disordered fragments flash
from sudden gas pump, scurrying car,
and momentary sign, to snatch

us briefly back into a creed
we have no further need to hold,
for life has pulled its curtain back
and we look out upon an old

and endless knowledge, time and form
all shifting entities of light,
and every mile ahead a mile
already travelled on our flight

from birth to death a hundred times;
slowly we turn down to the sea
from which we rose, and it is ice
and stretches to infinity.

That Was in Another Country
for Alexandru Engler

It was upon this hillside.
                    She is dead.

Suddenly I find I've lost her name
among these houses where once copses climbed
past nailed forbidding notices that kept
a different excitement near enough
to add a sharper colder risk to those
she taught me how to take.

Her hair was red.
I can't recall her age,

or do not wish
somewhere or other in me to be sure
she'd learned so much so young,

though now I feel
these child-packed houses huddled round the hill
she only had another year to share
are partly monuments

and make amends.

In the Woods

I didn't stop to read
the notice board.

Now I've a thought:
it could have said *Keep Out*

and listed penalties
if one should trespass,

so I may be a trespasser
round here

and perhaps the only one.
I've not yet seen

a sign of any other,
nor the owner

if he or she is
living in the house

I've kept away from,
glimpsed it big and calm

sometimes through trees
but sheered off not to face

the questioning stare,
What are you doing here?

or, maybe, from a
gripping hand a welcome

I've not earned,
though sometimes I've a mind

to take the risk,
and yet if they should ask

why am I here
I do not have an answer.

I could say I have lost
my memory, twist

my cap in nervous hands;
I could pretend

I'm hunting for a missing
child, could ring

the changes on that theme,
say I've no home

and that I'm lost.
I think I have been lost

in here for days
or years, and yet not lost

completely for
it seems familiar air

and everywhere I turn
there is a stone,

a flower, a leaf, a stream
that spells my name

so strangely that
I feel I am a part

of something, have a right
to be here, yet

why is there no-one else?
I peer through trees.

The Land

After a time
the land is not
outside you,
but a part of where
you deeply breathe
and firmly walk
the dark interiors
of your bones,

recording and
recalling all
the shames and triumphs
of the will
that moves the mountains
and the trees
and that the trees
and mountains move.

After a time
the land is not
where you have come
but where you are,
and every stone
upon the earth
is one more portrait
of your face,

sublime, indifferent,
or sad,
or cracking in that
sudden smile
with which you answer
travellers
that wash the history
from their bones.

Haystack Rock
for Sylvia and Brigid

This rock is metaphor; it lifts
up through a band of grey and silver mist
its vast bird-haunted breast as if, once Earth
were tilted, sky would nuzzle there to suck.

I trudge towards it, held upon my course
as if it were a lodestone, I the pin.
Ahead, sand is a mirror slick as ice
to teach the clouds to skid, the morning walkers
to slip through the surface to themselves,
and, as I cross that shine to steadier sand,
I pause at stretchmarks on the tightened skin,
at scars left by the scalpel tracks of birds,
and weals from whips of lost initiations,
and the rock looms closer, closer, till
the sky is almost filled with it, and I
am one of many scattering at its base;
men, women, children come here as a tribe
comes to the call from all their varied creeds,
and wander lonely, mindless through the crowd.
A crow steps delicately between two pools,
the black head jerking at each printed sign;
a white gull perches on the highest peak,
and, over there, where soon the tide will turn,
two boys bruise knees into a cavern shaped
threefold, a triple aperture in time
and space and breath; I wait for their return,
fearful of depths of darkness; they come back

small as the winking pink in this round pool
I find my feet by. And now, farther up,
another boy stands tall against the sky.
I envy him that careless arrogance
which I have lost, as I have also lost
the way into the cavern and the way
to walk back undisturbed to common shores,

having myself become a metaphor.

Moonshot
for Jack Kidder

There's the moon that men
have set their feet on.

Machines have walked it,
scrabbling up the rocks,

and cameras have
recorded it in colour,

sensors found it to be
dead in space,

no life at all, no air,
no fire, no water.

no earth you could call earth.
It moves round, dead

as any doornail. This is
absolute fact,

or would be that,
could facts be absolute

as this moon shining on us,
moving tides

and moods and minds and
altering the blood,

the trees, the dreams,
the ways we feel and move

together as we see Her
sail the skies.

House in a Clearing

1.

The dream invents existence,
its dimensions

challenging the house,
the trees, the mountain.

Waking, we shudder,
hug the shadows round us

against the cold, the heat,
the deafening landscape.

2.

In the nearby tree
a flicker, orange-winged:

I dare not leave
the vulnerable house.

Flame taps in my mind.
Flame eats my timbers.

Is there no rhyme
to make it fly away?

3.

The page ends.
It always ends.

And yet the mind,
continuous ribbon,

spreads, spreads
an endless message

covering the summer earth
like snow.

The Barrens
(Triolets)

Over the wilderness we go,
accepting space and time and death

that alter all we think we know.
Over the wilderness we go,

the ice, the tundra; here below,
trapped in the ultimate of breath,

over the wilderness we go,
accepting time and space and death.

We move towards the final chill,
accepting death and time and space

which are the climax of the will;
we move towards the final chill

of every impulse we fulfill
by travelling this emptied place.

We move towards the final chill,
accepting death and time and space.

It is the ultimate we serve,
accepting space and time and death,

the distance between nerve and nerve.
It is the ultimate we serve

through love and terror that observe
the chill declensions of the breath.

It is the ultimate we serve,
accepting space and time and death.

Sanctuary

It is a sanctuary. I stared
at the sand,
at the eggs
in the small hollow,

suddenly scared at my
wish. *Terns.*
I heard it 'turns'
and felt a turning

in me somewhere,
a slow curve
coming round
without an end

or a beginning,
a single turn
I must not touch.
I knew the law:

Don't touch the eggs,
disturb the birds.
I felt that I
disturbed the birds;

they were so quick
and light and went

away and something
other went

away in them.
Now, come away.
I came away,
and yet I stayed

with that curve in my
mind, that sense
of swerve, of
untouched altering,

which, like the law,
I still protect,
and, too, that frightening
sanctuary.

One Point on the Map

Here we believed.
Some places
escaped this
intense greed

for love and suffering,
never held
their own with an old
unforgiving wrong

or laid out stones
for murderous hands,
judicial minds,
but here, once,

there was belief,
a stern trust
in a true ghost
and a dead life

burdening this
with its hurt need
its choked blood.
We cannot pass

over it lightly.
The air is thick
with all that work
of God and holy

not with His presence
but with man's
long-lost conviction,
an intense

terror and peace,
an alarmed faith
that stopped the breath.
You share this place.

Limits

Everywhere there are limits,
barriers, boundaries,
shorelines, rivers, ditches,
fenceposts, crossings
that one must not cross,
foods one can't eat,
and even words one dare not
speak. This earth
is parcelled out among us
and each man
must live within his
portion. This is mine.
You're welcome to
explore it, as I do,
continually.
        Here's
my apple tree,
and here wife, daughter, dog,
and over there

a group of ghosts
not speaking to each other
but by way of me,
and, up beyond
that red brick house,
a copse, a pool, a broken
white horse lying on
harsh concrete, snapped
off at the thigh.
Why don't you look around,
see for yourself?

I see for myself now,
and it's a great
improvement upon seeing
just for other people
who can't see
(they say) without me,
though they'll have to learn,
as I have, through the years,
that there are limits
upon sharing
as on pain and love
and understanding,
not to mention time,
which I am always mentioning
like a clock
that makes the round trip
of its boundaries over,
over, over, over,
till it stops
at one fencepost for ever.
I don't know
where I would soonest
stop, but all too soon
I know I'll have to,
stilled within my limits
that won't feel like
limits any more,
but crossings that one crosses,
words one speaks.

ARE YOU LISTENING?

&

The Good Reason

I start the poem with you
for a good reason.

Now you are in the poem
and looking out

the poem has become a mirror
or a pool–

the poem itself prefers me
to say pool–

showing you yourself.
No other meaning

troubles the poem (or the pool).
It is very simple.

Here in the poem you are looking
at yourself reading,

and you are reading of how
you look from the poem–

I should say pool, but whether
pool or mirror

it is you that is looking down,
you looking up–

and you are the only reason
I made the poem.

Choice

I choose the words
that I am chosen by.
Have you the time
to listen for a time?

The words I say
are less than what I say;
the space between them
is a space of dark.

I need to shape these words
to shape my need.
I do not know my need,
I only know
the way towards it:
will you come my way
for this brief time?
The time is always brief.

The time is always brief
and always time.
Have you heard darkness yet?
I think I heard
one footfall in that pause.
Now let me pause
a little longer, hear
that little sound

that is the space between,
the chosen space
I did not choose
but I am chosen by,
and it is this I need–
or do I need
to think it so
because I need to think

beyond my words
because the words are mine
and will not let me share
as I would share
a common speech with you?
The only speech
we learn together
is the dark we learn

from listening, quiet.
Are you listening now?
The stillness nears.
I near you in this moment.

The Request
for Julia

You ask me to teach you.
I have taught

so little to so many
that I find

myself disturbed.
Must I again pretend

the wisdom of the
pebble and the rose?

Must I speak out
as if I were the sea

evoking thunders in
the hollowed rock

or blind you with the science
of the sand

downspilling from the carved
and wind-lashed dunes?

Must I, indeed, profess
an understanding

that can be transferred
from me to you

so simply, so directly,
over months

of wordy meetings,
careful dialogue?

Or shall I say that
everything I teach you

(apart from simple skills)
is all you know

already but pretend
you do not know

the better to be taught
and to find freedom.

In This Poem I Am

And in this poem I am,
Whoever else I am,
                    – W.S. Graham, *The Dark Dialogues*

First Poem

In this poem I am
someone you meet outside
the public library. He
is carrying a small book
which he has not yet read.
His hands are blue with cold.
He tells you his wife is buying
new drapes for the winter.

He is not important.
You do not have to mind
anything that he says.
It is only talk
to make smoke of the breath.
He stamps his feet. It is
November in Oak Bay.
Even the trees are shuddering.

In this poem I am
making smoke of the breath.
It shows me I am saying
something. What it is
does not matter. All
that always only matters
is what we have still to learn
and that we try to speak

to each other still
in spite of the bitter cold
frosting the fallen browns
of leaves in an Oak Bay .
that only differs from
your other place in being
where we meet and chat,
together in this poem
to stamp our feet and clutch
the books we have not yet read.

Second Poem

In this poem I am
walking through Beacon Hill Park.
The pond is frozen. Ducks
are walking upon the ice,
shuddering their blacks and greens.
A woman in fur-lined boots
is casting crumbs. A dog
is walking on its own.

You want the other poem?
The one in which I am
the voice of God? I think
it is too cold for that.
I have just come in
from the fine chill of the park.
Wait a moment while
I put the coffee on

and clear my throat. It is
a poem I do not like
to live in very much.
I get a little deaf
listening to those words
that God might overhear,
and though He understands
the fix that I am in

I shouldn't push my luck.
Can't I say in this poem
I am the way you sit
expectant in that chair,
your legs crossed and your hand
upon your rocking knee,
hoping for something good?
I hope for something good.
Almost I found it there
walking in Beacon Hill Park.

Third Poem

In this third poem I am
someone you expect.
I hear you say 'At last!'
I guess I ought to blush
but only stamp off snow
and lay my boots aside.
Your room is dark and warm.
I don't know who you are.

This is the usual thing.
I guess you'll understand
that when I come myself
I'm often rather shy
and clumsy with my feet.
Don't put away the cat.
There's no need for a fuss.
I'm sure my welcome's warm.

In this poem I am
at least no sad surprise,
familiar at least.
You've heard it all before
a number of good times
(I hope the times were good).
Your face is rather flushed.
Perhaps I'm not quite right?

Well, we all make mistakes.
I mean not to be more
or less than you expect,
but often there's a change
between the knock (or ring)
and greeting who comes in.
I always come in slow;
it gives time to adjust
as we (shall we?) adjust.
You must know what I mean.

Transmissions

This is a space
between spaces,
a far dimension
imitating timelight.

* * *

Note for a poem:
a bird falls
in the chasm between the keys
of the piano.

* * *

Identity:
the device and the delusion
from which stems
each dark polluted glory.

* * *

This house is a space
in which to discover
that space is a house.

* * *

Can any of you
suggest a way to draw
with sand upon water,
with mirrors inside glass?

* * *

Authority negates
both will and instinct;
will and instinct authorize
form, not law.

* * *

I can foretell
the elements of listening
in tomorrow's stillness,
but not the words.

Poem With a Phrase
By Robert Graves

You never know.
It might be this one that

sets him to dreaming
or undoes her blouse;

you just can't tell
the way things will turn out

when you begin to play
with words like this.

hopeful, but not too
hopeful, only certain

that something unexpected's
bound to happen,

like this butterfly
that's wandered in

and wandered out,
a flying-crooked gift

from someone else's poem,
(and you know whose),

but where's it got to now?
And will she care?

And will he leave a
happiness in the house?

The Hard Core

1.

This poem is erotic.
Do not read it
if you are under fifteen
or Mrs. Whitehouse.

It is presenting a
lady in black leather
holding a riding
crop, all set to bring it

down upon the naked
pearly buttocks
of a flushed submissive
girl who quivers

with anticipation—
a quite common,
even banal, scene,
but poems are never

quite this commonplace;
their core is harder.
Look closely. Note the chair,
the rug, the curtains

that are all
familiar, are all yours,
and at the window
your face weeping in.

2.

This poem is just as
erotic as the first,
so enter it with caution.
In this room

a naked girl is putting
on a raincoat
to the sound of
tinny violins,

and a man is taking
down his trousers,
displaying what you
customarily expect,

and, smiling, she has
moved onto the bed,
and now he is
possessing her. And yet

something is not quite right.
His thrust, her rapture
and the climactic moment
seem off-key,

perhaps because it
takes place in the bedroom
you have made the
nursery for your children.

3.

Now you know the trick
and are relaxing.

This poem won't surprise you
with your face,

your furniture, your children,
will not move you,

make you feel that
mocking twinge of guilt,

however gross it grows.
You are prepared.

The poem, too, is prepared,
is wholly naked,

calling to you from
the room beyond,

and, try hard as you can,
you won't get in.

Thinking It Out

Someone else is thinking
out these lines

as I am thinking them
and I should know

that it is you, but do I?
Is it you

or someone other?
You cannot be sure

enough to answer me
or you would answer,

and I'd hear it
somewhere in the poem

that I am thinking out
as someone thinks

along with me. Who thinks
along with me?

It could be a third
person; someone other

than the both of us
(if you are here)

could say this as I say it,
pause this pause,

attempt, indeed, this
nearing, here, conclusion

which is not the end.
Someone has made it

not the end, and was it
you? In thinking

out these lines I think
that I am thinking

less and less and finding
more and more.

Don't Worry About It

It's no big deal
but good enough for me.

I rather like the
easy feel of it,

the unimportant
casual way it moves

on down the page,
not bothering its head

about what people think
or think they think,

though it's the unimportant
things that matter

sometimes when we're
lonely or afraid–

the slow turn of her head,
his little cough,

the truly ugly picture
from back home–

still, this is unimportant:
you've no need

to read it any further
or at all

unless you like the
easy way it moves

and don't much care
if it is good enough.

Mnemonic

Even you will remember
a little of this.

Not perhaps the words–
you, little, remember–

but the twist of a phrase,
the way it twisted

round, its tail in its mouth,
its mouth on its tail,

as if (remember, will you?)
even of this

little gesture a mystery
has been born

and something beautiful
because a mystery

is most beautiful when
partly lost

and lost partly when
beautiful because

we dare only remember
a little of this.

Trio

Expect
little

Hope
much

Dream
the

Impossible

* * *

a green silk
leaf a

red silk
leaf a

buckle of
sun

October

* * *

Born by the
sea,
     my
hands
still

twitch
     when the
wave
breaks
     an
     in-
visible
line.

FRIENDS AND STRANGERS

✿

At the Door

Do I know you?
Come in, anyway.

We don't stand on
ceremony here,

and every stranger's
welcome as the flowers

in the Spring, though I
won't sing Tra-la

as Martyn Green did–
you remember him?

I guess not. We all have
such different memories

but for the first one;
that at least we share

with death and love,
so come in, anyway.

Kanata

Only a neighbour knows
the place you know.

You can trust him
with a nod or drink,

a single word, a
gesture; only he

will understand the
birthcry in the house,

the sudden laughter
and the quiet death,

or be the exact
enemy you need.

Therefore be wary
of the smiling stranger;

even in his knowledge
and his love

he has not learned
the stillness of the door

that only murmurs
in a Sunday wind.

At the Fair

Back at the old stand?
Yes, he said,
back at the old stand!
That was it–
a certain wryness,
a grim acceptance,
resignation become a habit

as for all of us.
Here, now,
seeking Her out in the deep cavern
back of the mind,
the heart, the gut,
hopeful and fearful,
I have to say it,

Back at the old stand.
She, maybe,
hearing me, knowing me
questioning, near,
may say the same,

hold out Her hand,
flame in the fingers,
almost touch

and then withdraw
as in the past,
(or was it the future?)
time on time.
Nothing much changes
as we change.
We follow light
and the light follows.

Brothers

One holds his own
with broken lumber
black with rain,

building it round
his days of waiting,
studying the sound

inwardness of it,
the grain and shine
when it will be split.

The other faces
the spread of death
in brown dried grass,

the balding yard
of his hard summer
staring ahead

at a bad winter.
The one whistles
in clinging air,

planning the steel
incision, the fling
and scream of the wheel

scattering out light.
The other thinks
he might as well sit

this year out,
and the next, and the next.
They do not write

but sometimes phone.
They are getting on
about alright.

The Appointment

The girl in the glass
is painting her face.
She is eager to please.

She has not thought
very much about death.
It's too soon for that.

The ring on her finger
is new and bright.
She brushes her hair.

Outside in the street
the man in the car
is enjoying the night.

He toys with a scarf
on the vinyl seat.
It should be quite safe.

He has not thought
very much about life.
He is past all that.

Wayfaring

They've gone on.
I watched them pass
me on the road.
I'd stopped to lean

against a gate.
A man must learn
once in a while
to lean and wait

for nothing in
particular as
it helps to get
the meadow mown

if someone's leaning
there and I
will gladly lend
a hand to bring

the harvest home,
however far
they get before
I travel on

to greet their banter
with a grin,
the last man at
the feast of winter.

In the Hills

Though he was born
right by this creek,
you'll hear him talk
of *the old country*
and making a visit
one of these days,

scratching under
his battered stetson

as if to get it
settled, yet
he's never known it
or left the farm,

so why *Old Country*,
why *Old?*
In what way?
He'll shake his head.

It's always been
the Old Country.
His grandfather
crossed the sea

in eighty five
as a young man;
his father was wounded
on the Somme;

what would *I* call it?
I don't know.
One of these days
he'll up and go.

Stopping Off
for Christopher Wiseman

I stop off here.
Back in a minute.
A thing to deliver,
then we'll get on.

How often I've heard it.
A farmyard gate.
Hedge clustering chickens.
He'll be gone

five minutes, ten.
Poured me a cup;
couldn't say no.
Her girl's sick.

or *Got a new Calf.*
Had the shed painted.
Gathering me eggs.
when I get back

from stopping off here,
reckon I'll say
Couldn't say No.
I was bloody drafted:

A couple of wars,
and then the kids.
No way of leaving,
avoid offended

looks, climb back,
and on we'll go.
How long before
the long job's ended?

Imprisoned
for George Faludy

1.

Not in the stone-scarred gaol
but in the solid flesh
that fastens up us all,

solitude has become
a presence, neither he
nor she, within the room.

We speak but may not touch.

2.

Uncertain just where we
may actually be,
I grope and fantasize.

I have been told there is
a here and now of earth,
but grasp no certainty,

for every time I stare
out of the window, there
is yet another place

and my companion seems
assured that even Time's
a blowing seed of grass.

3.

I can't claim torture save
that of the pinioned mind
deliberately deprived,

and as the years go on
(if I can trust in years)
the dull continuation

of the term I serve,
but cannot know how long
or what I have deserved.

4.

I do not call it age
but gradual release
and page by page by page

attempt to scribble down
the sparse inquiet facts.
that whispers have made known,

such as: A hand can heal;
a mind can reach outside;
a stone can think and feel;

such as: Time has its holes
through which a man may pass;
such as: all things are soul.

5.

It comes to me that I
have made this prison here,
and made it out of fear.
If I escape I die,

and I have made of death
a truth I cannot face,
a place that is no place,
an ending of the breath

I too absurdly trust.
It comes to me that life
pins death down like a knife
and that the knife will rust.

Not Grief But Thanks

I have heard you are
dead. You should have told me
yourself. I would have listened.
I've heard news
of you quite often—
this poem or that poem
strutting an Ottawa street,
glimpsed in a bar
scratching its grey but
still surprising head—
and always paid attention.
You should have told me
how it was, who took you.
Did it turn

out to be the Angel
you had promised
both of us? Or was it a
crisp white doctor
with pale hands, hooded eyes?
You must have died
quite quietly, or I'd have
heard that thin
firm carrying voice,
and also at some distance
from us here: Quebec,
the Yukon, Prince
Edward Island–that
could be the place
to end, a princely ending,
not Moose Jaw,
breath choking, teeth ajar....
Or did you plan
not telling me, manoeuvring me
to surprise
myself with it, this lack of
grief, this notion
that your having left
where once you were
has placed you here more nearly
than quite since
we rubbed poems last.
We're rubbing poems again
here now, for yours are all
the places mine
are speaking, being
everywhere, as once
you said they'd be at death
blessed by truth's Angel.

The Clowns

Clowns are serious
people. They derive
assurance from their
failures. She, in love
with loving, finds it
harder to confess
her claims on dignity
ridiculous,
and, over cocktails,
it is *Simply Heaven*
to be here together!
I respond
appropriately. Her
costume is *Divine*
and she is looking
Marvellous. We lie
to illustrate the truth,
to shape the real
and raw absurdities
for which we fool,
and, having all, lack
nothing but our selves,
or so it seems. We've
learned the ways to seem
and do not boggle at
dishonest truth.
I let my history starve
outside her door;
she puts a muzzle on
the nightmare's breath;
and we are in Romance.
Yet when she turns
her head I see the
child I never knew,
and if I groan I glimpse
a blundering fear,
directionless as moths.
The light shines through
the patches on our scene.

Another sun
has hurts and freedoms where
we'll never come,
pathetic, confident.
Her make-up blurs.
The tears upon the mask
are human tears.

Elbows
for Barbara Turner

There are elbows
one will never know,

never see bracing their
sharpness on a table,

never see changing from
smooth to wrinkle to smooth,

never even catch with a
gasp in the ribs,

but there are always
warm familiar elbows

also, bony, plump, pale,
flushed, soft, rough,

to provide one with the
needs one needs,

the changing shapes of need,
the jutting bones.

The Book

First a photograph
of the author smiling,

then the words, the pages
and pages of words,

the words indenting the paper
ever so slightly

and carrying colons and commas
and semi-colons

along with them in their flow
like riverborne leaves

fallen from some madrona
leaning over

hurrying scurrying water,
then one empty

page revealing the weave
of the paper, white

as earth before the thaw
that set the river

running. End or beginning?
Close the book.

Observe the photograph
of the author smiling.

The Reception

She knows who I am.
Her smile is broad,
her handclasp warm.
We must have had a drink
together sometime.
We have not been to bed.
That, at least, I know.
What does she know?

I feel a twinge of
jealousy. Her memory
is so much better than mine,
and, it seems, warm.
Who are her friends? '
She isn't with any friends.
Should I know her name,
and did I, ever?

I say *I had better mingle,*
and move away
with an expression I hope
looks like regret.
It well might. I am,
after all, regretful.
I have missed out on
something I haven't missed.

Poems are easier.
I know who I am
for them, in them,
by the third verse at worst,
and even if I'm not
the man I was,
I am almost the man
I'm going to be

before it's over,
if it doesn't stop
midway in career

as now I stop
looking across the room
to see that she
is someone else,
and rather else than someone.

The Fact Of It

I have to say I knew him.
That's a fact.

But he was not the sort of
fact one knows:

tall, slightly stooping, Roman
nose, a head

of some dead sated
Emperor, a voice

of dark fur, padding claws,
a gentle smile

part self-absorbed, part questing,
part supreme

self-confidence and yet
sometimes aslant

and nervous. In his
long dark overcoat

he never stood, but loomed;
he never sat

but was enthroned or
fastened to a chair

by inner steel-eyed
sorcerers, his hands

locked on the inexplicable,
intense,

his heavy lidded gaze
upon his knees,

his shoes, my shoes, the space
between us. Yes,

I knew him. He knew me.
That fact's exact.

Changing

I knew or thought I knew you
but you are changing

as, here, I am changing
like the leaves,

the trees, the grass.
It is, you say, their nature,

as it is my nature,
but you change

more slyly, wantonly.
You alter time

and history and belief
to place your face

within a different mirror
and you turn

down other darker roads
than those I know

to farther destinations
as I change

my own slow footsteps,
move another man

down from the bedroom
to a different dawn.

Two Sides of the Record

1. *for Clive Rippon*

No-one has ever
heard them but myself.
That's untrue, but it's
the way I feel,
looking over the labels,
Nellie Lutcher,
Mr Goon Bones, Billy Kyle,
Red Allen,
names that give me back
something that went
away from me, although
exactly when
I can't say. It was
when I also lost
a kind of innocence
I haven't missed
until this evening,
for as they begin
to spin I sense a second
phantom needle
moving from periphery
to centre
within timeless grooves
cut in the darkness
contributing a different
colder sound.

2. *for Arlene Lampert*

The needle spirals
inward on the black
and glistening record of
what I last heard
in wartime barracks,
and my feet tap as
they tapped then in
the Other Ranks Canteen
as if to dance down boredom
and the ever
present unacknowledged
wordless fear
that went with the
neighborhood. I didn't
know the name of the band
or who was singing
but I know now
and alter recollection,
saying
Tony Pastor
as if he
and I were old familiars,
which we were
in some sense, I suppose;
we shared this shining
spinning dark
from which the needle draws
the rocking tapping dance,
but not the silence
following; in that
we moved apart.
as we move now apart,
I and that boyhood.

Running On

We are all of us running
out of time. You can see
us there on the level stretch
of the high moor, black
against the pale sky, running
one by one by one;
it almost looks like a dance.
And you, of course, are running

also. You can see
yourself, the familiar face
in profile, the half clenched hands,
the rising and falling feet
still in their usual shoes.
If you were up above
on the high tor you'd get
a different picture, see

not the familiar face
but the awkward bobbing head
you do not know so well,
while from the little strearn
below the track you'd look
up at another thing,
hardly a person at all,
just moving feet, the face

the neck, the jaw, the head
hidden quite from view.
Each viewpoint brings one more
impression, but the best,
of course, is on the run
itself. You do not see
yourself from there at all
but only the one ahead

who does not take the view
that he is running out
of time at all. He swears
it's time that is running out

and is about to end,
and then there'll be no then
or any way to run,
or speak, or even view

the world which will be out
of money, luck and breath
as are you now? I am,
almost, but keep running.

Just a Moment
for Carl & Hilda Morris

A ceremony? You could say that
if it were not to dignify
the small occasion beyond sense.

I guess you, too, could call it custom,
but not ritual. It is not
a worshipping or celebration

but how we choose to give each meal
a kind of order, linking hands
like this around the supper table

in a silence hardly longer
than the pause between two words
in ordinary talk, one moment

of the day, one simple moment
simply passed. You could say that.

Three Portraits of Susan

I.

Layer upon layer
the rock shelves,
shuffled and slanting,
hold her here

in a hand woven
heavy skirt
and a black shawl;
bare armed,

seated on rock,
she hugs her knees
with stiff hands.
Her hair is thick.

a spreading mane,
her jaw strong,
her eyes dark
as the dark scene

of stone and mist
at the land's edge,
silver burdening
her thin wrist,

her mouth proud;
above her head
dead grass shudders
to the wind.

II.

The tree behind
her is seamed, old.
Her long-boned hands,

holding a beaded
thong, are ringed;
her hair is braided

indian fashion,
her tunic fringed.
Some bark has broken

away, left scars.
Her face is calm,
the tired eyes

gazing beyond
us, beyond place,
the set mouth sad.

III.

Her shawled arms laid
across her knees,
she sits on the ground,

skirt trailing in leaves,
light falling through leaves
bringing shadows of leaves

to pattern her long
white hands, her pale
half-turned face gazing

down at the leaves,
the thin twisting leaves
in the shadow of leaves.

Friend

Friend, if I may
call you friend

and send you this
along the page

and through the
passages of time,

forgive my being
separate

in place, in time.
I would not be

so distant but
I am of earth

whose creatures cannot
help or shed

the shyness of
particular skin

and I must keep
this distance or

deny what both of us
apart

can only understand
apart,

the need to speak
and to be secret.

L.S. Lowry Aged Seventy Two

Big-boned, shabby,
a great neb of a nose,
he grinned down at her
tautly swollen belly.
'Your first?' 'No. One of
eighteen months.' Eyes bright
'They'll fight,' he said, and
then again, 'They'll fight!'

And I remembered
the painting, two men black
in big boots in grey streets
watched by thin women,
children, railings, and a
boarding house,
the black of boots, the black
of chimney stacks.

Now after twenty years,
he long since dead,
I hear that dry voice,

see that great nebbed face
bent peering down,
a sly and truthful prophet
old as Adam, smiling
on the children,
telling Eve *They'll fight.*
Oh yes, they'll fight!

Why Should the Novelists Have All the Fun?

In this book you are
red-lipped in furs

beside me on a sleigh.
I'll be your husband

before the night is out.
The driver, huddled

from the cold is
urging on the horses

through the twilit
whiteness of a world

you have kissed mine.
Or, if you are a man,

then you are holding her
and I am urging

on the horses. In
each case we're threatened

all three of us by
other following travellers

in black cloaks with
brightly gleaming teeth

and terrible intentions.
I am happy

(are you happy?)
in this love and danger

because of the next
chapter, for I've read

ahead--it always pays
to read ahead--

and know we'll cross
the bridge before it falls.

Death of a Mouse

It was a small death
silently met
in a warm night.

Morning came
with a sad mouth
telling a truth

we did not need
in our busy home.
Run out of time

on the scurrying wheel,
he no longer hid
his head or burrowed

under the papery
shavings, curled
plump from the real

hardness of light,
but, humped, lay
lost as a cry

in the wide cage.
One comes to expect
no less of fate

than Finis. It
is a turned page,
a different pledge.

Your Mistake

In a bright blue skirt and a red blouse
she is making pastry,

rolling it out on the board,
the small hairs glistening

on her forearms, her buttocks
clenched and sturdy,

her feet a little apart.
She is not my wife.

My wife is someone else.
She brushes back

a tendril of light blonde hair
and sprinkles flour

on the pale brown board,
(she is not my daughter),

her full breasts rising and falling;
She is humming

softly under her breath.
She is not my lover.

The Guardians
for Carl and Hilda Morris

1.

Three bronze figures
stand before the house
on its brown platform
in the restless trees,
gaudy with lichen
and with moss, the birds
darting about them,
on a black-sparred pine
red nectar for the hummingbird
and wild bee,

and here I have come
once more to reach
into the grandeur
of a dream
fulfilled in rivers
and in trees
and dark-veined looming
rocks, and, high
above us, eagles
drifting slow
across the black miles
of the pines,

and here I have come
again to touch
the permanence
that lives within
each one of us
and is this land
and built this house
that you have built.

2.

Nightlong we talk,
turn, pause, and counter-turn
bringing us always
to one faith, one doubt.
*Perfection of the life
or of the work?*
Or is the life the work,
the work the life,
the inward knowledge?

Outside in the rain
the three bronze guardians
glisten, window-lit,
and shadows move them
as if they would dance,
but suddenly from the west
the nightwind roars
and we, remembering
dark mortality,
and the recurring dream,
lurch to our beds
still answerless
beneath the timeless trees.

3.

We break our night fast
by the window, watch
leaves shaking as a chipmunk
skitters, jumps
platform to pine
and vanishes. I know
that swift assurance
an intelligence.
A hummingbird, stilled wingless
in a blur
of blue and crimson, dips
his beak. I see
the poise of passion
and the seed of time.

He dips, then sideslips off;
the thought is gone,
but reappears,
a raindrop on a thorn
that clings, fills, gathers,
swollen with the light,
then drops to shatter,
vanishing. I look
up at the boughs.
Another raindrop forms.

Where are the gods?
Must we hunch through the books
upon these dark stained shelves
to find their names?
Can we not learn the answer
from the land
that feeds us, breeds us, buries us,
and holds
this house and household firm,
or should we turn
simply to these three guardians
at our door,
Clotho, Lachesis, Atropos?
I stare
beyond the trees
and high up in the sky,
the eagle Zeus,
the sun god, and the sun....

4.

It was, I now recall–
do I recall
or do I fantasize?–
between these trees
I stood and heard
within an owl's call
the tension of the heartstring
and the pain
of climax in the body
and the soul

combined, and then
the sudden wingbeat down
through black flanged pines
to where I clutched my breath
small under tangle,
knowing that my breath
was in that sound,
encompassed by that sound,
and my identity another I,
which nears me now,
the nightlong talk no more
than memories of a hand
that gripped a hand
above the drinks,
the shared improvidence
and passion, and the mutual
endless urge
that these three guardians know
yet do not know.
They watch us, dawnlit,
as we grope for light.

5.

Let me put it simply.
We are trapped
in an endeavour
in which none succeeds.
Let me be brutal:
we are animal;
our folly is to think
we own the sky
and can explain it.
What is to explain?
It simply is the edge
of where we are
and we are at the edge.
We have climbed here,
and it has taken
fifty, sixty years,
and now we look down

from the edge and back
away; we cannot
see what we have seen.

6.

It is a day of rain;
the rain sweeps down,

each leaf, each needle,
gathering, filling, loosing

threads of rain until the
threads of rain

have woven curtains
between here and sky.

And now we fill our
coffee mugs, remark

upon the headlines,
by your hand a bronze

dark Chanticleer
that you have made, and by

your head a vivid timeless
chart of time

that you have painted
with the soul's conviction.

the fingers' sureness;
now we are not sure.

The guardians outside
are soot and shade,

impervious, abstract, permanent.
I scratch

the table with a pin.
Wood thrusts. Pin bends.

7.

Begin again:
three figures at the door
upon the platform
in the trees
beneath the wooden rafters
daubed
with lichen and with moss,
the birds

red-throated, blue-winged,
gold and green,
darting about them,
on a pine
red nectar
for the hummingbird
and the wild bee,
and at one side

a trestle table
and a bench
weathered black
by sun and storm;
here I have come again
to talk
daylong and nightlong
over wine,

and here I have come
again to learn
that we may never learn
who seek,
and that the gods
of permanence
are shifting as
these words we speak.

Busy
for Sylvia

I was going to tell you ...
but it will keep.

Your hands are busy with fingers,
your mouth with smiles,

and the dog has discovered a flea,
and the rose is dropping

petals one by one
in a busy wind

that has the trees in a tizzy.
It's not the time

to tell you what I meant to
tell, and, too,

it doesn't matter now.
It will never matter

more than your smiles and fingers,
and it will keep.

FIVE FOR CALLIGRAPHERS

&

The Calligraphy Lesson
for Pamela Barlow Brooks

I am learning to write
again. I forgot
that it was hard,

pulling the lines
down, round, and shaping
the places they meet,

the spaces they lessen
and widen, the
way they are tall

and eager or huddled
and squat, the
way that they spell

not how I hear it
or say it
or even think

but in a fashion
they choose,
describing a track

through silence,
in silence,
            answering
the loud world back.

The Start
for Pamela Barlow Brooks

First of all
remember
how to draw

as a child
knows how to draw,
the letters

being life
itself, not
merely letters

but ghosts and
birds and beasts
upon the page

and wind and waves
and fire and, if
they alter

underneath your
hand, respect
the change,

admiring them
for thinking out,
like children,

what you did not
think and could not
spell.

I
For Bob Levine

Shaping it for
the first time
it feels easy,

hardly more
than one firm
stroke of the pen,

yet everything
depends on it;
without it

there would be
no written
speech at all,

nor any need
to speak, and
yet it's not

the first shape
to be made;
that is the moon's;

I follows after,
tree against
the moon,

man's finger on
the whiteness
of the page.

O
for Sylvia Skelton

O is the commencement
of all skill
and the initial
moment of the world.

O is the end
in which are all beginnings,
the pool from which
the words of music rise.

O is the meeting
of two motions in
the round and silver
mirror of the moon.

And O is emptiness,
the Tao, the Way,
the universe of our
surrounding sky.

The End
for Ann Hechle

Letter it carefully
in good black ink

and on white paper
by the melting light

of a single candle,
every stroke

of the pen a breath
and every pause

three breaths and only three
if you would have

intent become intensity
and power

move in music from
the speaking page.

MAKING THEM

 හ

Makar

With less to say
than rain on stone,
with more unknown
than loam and clay;

with less to tell
than stream and weir,
with more to fear
than pool and well;

with less to feel
than moving air,
with more to share
and more to heal

than beast or bird,
I put this word
upon this word
upon this word.

Something

Something is hidden
somewhere and peers out

at the thing called poet
and his universe

of words and words and words.
Something is waiting

for the words to stop
so it can be heard

breathing, breathing on
as if breath alone

were the essential
message, words and words

no more than gravel
thrown against the pane.

Speech

Speech is a part of me
I cannot help.

It is its own thing
as we say a man

is his own man,
deliberate, independent.

I know speech partly
from the way it moves

as cattle move,
sidelong, slow, hesitant,

edging towards what it
may come to say

if no-one shouts
or if the wind stays there

in the right quarter.
I know speech in part

also from what it carries
of old words–

wind stone, sea,
bone, stillness breath–

dusty with wear as
anglo-saxon churches

squarely sturdy in
rook-haunted trees

where first it spoke;
although I know sometimes

it does not care to
wear inheritance

as openly as that
and puts on vague

elaborations, even
grotesque manners,

attempting to disguise it
from itself,

and from me also,
always in the end

it gives that up, and
independent, slow,

edges its way
away from and towards

what there's to find out
in that silent world

it came to change,
and tell, and talk about.

The Arrangement

This is a new arrangement.
Sounds are here

and here and here,
the musics of the moon

made various in the
various lilting day

of pebbles, petals,
parapets and bees,

descants and harmonies;
I harmonize

a phrase, a further phrase,
a movement, move

the minims round,
the breves and semi-breves,

the bars, the rests,
and listen to my listening

as the wind to wings
that sweep and swerve

to seize the concerts
of the air and make

of gales a glory,
of disorder order.

In, Through, Out

I enter my room
and the poem
and am in a forest

stifled by bracken
stumbling
on leathery roots

knowing there could be
an accident
here in the poem

and i could be killed
i am killed
i am looking up

the narrowing trunks
to a blackness
of leaves against sky

and changing i change
i am earth
i am water and stone

and speaking as water
and stone i am
reaching the end

and beginning the
light of the sky at the
end of the poem

Closer Now

I am closer now
than ever before,

even though there are
oceans in between

and continents, more
continents than before,

and even though
I am older, older far

than She met
those centuries ago

if centuries have any
meaning left

for those whose separation
is not time's

but destiny's,
the raindrop and the rose,

the lightning and the tree.
I am more near

to Her than ever, now,
and more afraid,

more stirred by terror
and by happiness,

hunched, grey-haired,
above the altering verse.

Four Inscriptions

1.

I no longer seek.
I have been found.

God, have mercy;
lose me for a while.

2.

I am scared;
there is so much between us:

love, understanding, trust—
the great dividers.

3.

This is a secret;
keep it like a song:

songs are the only truly
hidden things.

4.

No-one is listening.
It does not matter.

I am making something
for far stars.

The Hermit Shell
for W. S. Graham

This is not
the simplest way
to say the thing
I mind hearing
between those rocks,
a slow shuffle
of tide clicking
the round stones,

and is not even
the right measure.
I speak this measure
against that
crash and drag
of the big tide
that shuffles pebbles,
indrawing breath

again to shout,
for it is when
the puny almost
mute syllables

counter the vast
onrush and surge
that time extends
what we have come from

into what we
here inherit
of the resistant
dying shell
hooked on perfection,
spiralling
constructions of
that inward sea

we learn, lifting
between rocks
the hermit's empty
house, our mouths
shaping the children's
O, the round
O between
contrary missions

of the particular
current, and
hear (do you hear?)
the small pulse
outthrob the greater,
dignified
by those tenacities
we share.

The Insistent
for Joe Rosenblatt

The poem insists on becoming
in spite of defeat.

It swells, looms, bursts through the
brown clay, pierces, shrills,

shudders to wind, spreads leaves wide,
plumps a bud

and opens up in front of
us. The poem

insists upon becoming
in spite of that

black fence, that tramped flat path,
that straying cat,

and our dismissal of its
point as pointless,

our defeat of it. It comes.
It blooms.

It spreads its petals, shouts at
us, and then

it dies into anthologies
like grass.

The Good Word

Dawn is a good word
but I let it pass.
Even for this poem
I cannot turn
the green light of the leaves
outside my window
grey and pale or phrase
the long faint shadows
on the worn brown planking
of the patio,
and yet it is so good
a word I cannot
leave it there alone
at the poem's beginning

but must say Dawn again
as these words move
slowly into the mind,
creating shadows.

On the Record
for Lawrence Russell

They have put my voice on a ribbon
to have it speak

when I'm not there,
or sick, or dumb, or dead,

along with other ribbons,
other voices;

they have called their collection
The Spoken Word,

and they have valued,
catalogued, insured

every ribbon; there are
miles and miles

of speaking voices
wholly disembodied,

deprived of the
necessity of breath,

the gulp and stretch of
muscle, heave of lung,

the fear, the arrogance,
and all these voices,

(mine there somewhere now,
a hurried voice

caught up in travelling time)
are speaking poems

that, whirring from one
spindle to another,

pass mortal frailties by
as if God's words.

Numbers

Buying a loaf is one
way to start counting,
making coffee another,
a third just walking
down the road to the pond
to watch ducks waddle
hieroglyphs in the mud.
It is very simple.
What begins is anything we think
feels like a beginning.
You can start
from a picked pin, a giggle,
a ridiculous bet,
even a good strong crap
or a vision of God.
Everything counts and adds
up to the name
you are and carry forward
line by line,
only changing the words
and not the poem.

Lost
for Kathleen Raine

Only the lost poem tells
the story true,

the poem that slipped
into a crack in time

and is now a wing that
never flew,

a hand that never touched,
a throat that strained

for speech but never spoke,
could not arrange

the cloak of language round
the naked light.

The Companion
for Margaret Blackwood

Companion to the poem,
not–not–its master,

but one that walks beside it
through dark trees

into the very heart
of the sacred grove,

disturbed by nearing
mysteries I must share,

I turn aside one moment
just one moment,

hesitant, and then
turn back to find

the desert all around
and my companion

little more than
footprints in the dust.

Minutiae

Such moments as these
most ordinary moments

in the cool dim house,
leaves shadowing glass,

doors open upon summer,
the hum and rattle

of the traffic far,
the book laid down,

are the most proper moments
to make poems

about such moments,
one required subject

of the Muse's rigorous
course of study,

but bringing neither
credits nor applause.

This Is

This is a space
I fill slowly

up with what we have
called words,

things that live and
work and pray,

come out of darkness
to extend

their blessing and
their wisdom through

the space that makes them
what they are,

that aeon between
sound and silence

in which their names
discovering Name,

perceive within that
Name the void

they now must heal,
they now must fill.

The Words

When the words have finished coming
look for the words

that are standing not quite out of sight,
a sidling, shuffling,

half uneasy herd that
snuffs the air,

suspicious of us, won't let
us come near

unless upwind and cautiously.
Be cautious.

These may be tomorrow's
words or words

that won't be seen again.
I walk upwind.

I glimpse them quick.
They see me and are gone

with a sudden kick and scutter.
But I climb

the hill to where they were,
search on the ground

for marks, for broken sticks,
crushed grass, black droppings

that might help me learn
their nature, guess

at least their habits,
if not track them down

across the country to their
desolate meanings.

Moving Right Along

Moving into this
I feel quite at home.

Tony is grunting
over his usual drink.

Mollie is calling the cat
in from the garden.

Bill and Sarah are laughing
in the kitchen.

Over the Olympics
the clouds are ruffled.

There is an empty car
parked by the bank.

Sylvia is appealing to
Saint Anthony

to discover her cheque book
and her keys.

Everything is easy,
moving along

in the way life moves.
There is nothing random.

The girl that smiles at me
is the girl that smiles.

The poem that speaks itself
is the poem that speaks.

Is Not and Is

A poem is not
an anecdote,

not a bald tale
baldly told;

nor is it
a hectic plot

that sets the players
gabbling prayers;

a poem is not
ingenious thought

or passionate stress:
it is a house

we recognize
as the one place

we have to live
until the grave.

The Poem

This is a public
place and far
from secret.

The gates are never
locked against
the curious.

Even at night
they are kept open.
Vandals

need not fear
arrest or
interruption

any more than
lovers or
wild children.

Come here any
time you wish.
You're welcome

to explore,
spread litter,
drink or fight.

It happens all
the time and
no-one's more

delighted than
the founder,
still alive

and watchful
in his winter
overcoat.

De Nihilo

I have nothing to say
today at all. It's nothing
more or less than nothing.
I wouldn't call it the Way,

The Emptiness, the Void.
I wouldn't even say
Nothing Will Come of Nothing,
for nothing has been said

to make me think or sense
that is the way to speak.
I might say Nothing's Perfect
and Nothing Is Left To Chance,

but even that could sound
both devious and obscure,
yet nothing is up my sleeve
and I have nothing planned,

believe me! Nothing's sure
but that I've nothing to say
and so there's nothing to fear
and nothing to endure.

Not in the Pity

After a while
the poetry does not matter,

if by that word we mean
that which allures,

for after a while
(in my case fifty years)

poetry becomes a
thinking-out of things

and yet itself a thing
that cannot think

but has to act out thinking
in a dance

precise and random as
the dance the atom

holds within its
infinite startling space,

or as the dance of Kali
swinging skulls

around Her throat until
they all are flowers.

A Word to the Wise

Those who ask excitement
of these words,

desiring vivid passions,
desperate vows,

the lunge of lovers
at the highest branch,

the cries of prophets
at the burning pyres,

should remember that
the river, tumbling

whiteness at its source
and in the Spring

of hurling waters, as it
nears the sea

runs deep and uneventful
to its home.

The Box
for Pat Martin Bates

There is a box on the table,
a brown wooden box.
It is, I suppose without measuring,
eight inches square,
indeed a cube. I know I am
altering the box
by putting these words down
but do not know
in what way I am altering it,
and the box
is altering me, though how
I cannot say,
nor how I was before I
saw the box.

This is boring stuff,
and, being boring,
alters in a fashion
quite distinct
from that it would

were I to interpose
some phrase about the
box exuding blood,
or even say whose name
is on the box.

We change and we are changed
in ways unknown
and by peculiar means—
that is peculiar
to the time, the place,
the thing, the person,
and, in this case, the page.
It is the page
not I that placed the box
upon the table.

The Inability

I cannot complete it
any more

than anyone can ever
hold a garden

steady, keep it
unchanged and complete.

It grows, it alters,
makes new moves, extends

itself, draws back,
is bright with falling shadows,

dark with stillness,
twilit by a mist,

echoing endlessly, or
filled with whispers

in a fashion I
cannot predict.

Guessing's no good.
I've tried it. Calculation's

quite incompetent
to even start

upon the problem—
if it is a problem;

it may, of course, be
rather more an answer

to the problem,
always incomplete,

changing, growing, without
start or end.

Making a Poem for Chistmas

Make me a poem for Christmas?
I make a poem

with lambs, a crib, some
shepherds and a child

that doesn't cry but
nestles in harsh straw

as if he were in bliss—
I'd say he was

at least six months;
somehow he won't come out

as crumpled pink and
dribbling as he should,

and she, the mother, is all
dressed in blue

and has a dazed expression.
I am dazed

myself and make another poem.
The poem

has three old men, two white,
one black, in robes,

each carrying a
jewel-encrusted box,

kneeling around a cradle,
and the child

now, surely, twelve months old,
is smiling, sweet,

both blue eyes focussed
perfectly, hair blonde.

It's no good. Everything
gets in the way;

the myths, the legends
carols, hymns, and prayers

roar louder than the
loudest army chorus

parading Disney figures
on the screen.

Surely there must be
another way:

poor people huddled from
the dreadful weather

in a stable smelling of
stale urine

cow-breath plumes upon
the frost-filled air,

and the baby swaddled up
so tight

only a small button nose
is showing,

and the mother
anxious and exhausted

lying back on straw,
her husband pacing

up and down, flapping
his arms and saying

"Maybe tomorrow you'll
be strong enough

and we can go on
and get out of this,"

she nodding wanly,
then the baby crying,

confused and fretful.
But you don't want that–

you want a celebration
and a paean

of praise, an organ tone
of moving sound,

or maybe crystal
tintinabulations,

flashing lights.
kaleidoscoping joy

upon the decked and laden tree,
and crackers

tugged, bang, with their
riddles and their mottoes,

and the turkey crisped
bright bronze and slicing

cleanly, with the sausages,
brussel sprouts,

baked potatoes, gravy,
then the lying

back in armchairs groaning
gently, stirring

now and then to eye
the fuzzy screen

and Tiny Tim godblessing us....
It's still wrong.

If I must make a
Christmas poem I must

make it much shorter
and say only:
        This

midwinter in the dark
time of the year,

give, and be thankful;
fill the house with light

to bring the light,
to bring the love, the peace

that story holds up to us
like a dream

from which we must not
ever fully wake

if years are to continue
on this earth.

WORDS FOR WITCHES

☙

Magic

Do not believe in magic;
there is nothing

magical in any
thing we do

if magic means a power
transcending nature;

all we do is natural
as the way

buds lean into the sun
and close in rain,

as natural as the
salmon-leaping stream,

the downswoop of the hawk
the loon's lone cry,

as natural as the
travelling of sound

and light, the magnet's pull,
the spin of earth,

the moon-tug on the tide,
the earthquake's heave,

the lightning and the
falling of the stars.

Yet if you call these
magical, believe

that magic is not
separate from the world,

but is the world,
and so believe in magic

as all of life and all
our hurrying lives.

The Rule

Only when it is
necessary; this

is the first rule of
magic. Do not cast

spells casually. Do not
curse or bless

unless your heart is
wholly locked on good

and not for you alone.
The second rule

is: Do not show the real
to be illusion

unless honest danger
force your hand,

entitling you to act
with personal power

as if yourself were
goddess or were god.

Initiate

Sealed Hers with perfumed
oil upon your forehead,

having dedicated
knife, cup, cord,

all working implements,
do not presume

the power a servant
at your beck and call

believing you must pay
lip-service only,

casually keeping
festivals by rote

and not within the
heart; it is a burden

you must bear in love
and pride through darkness.

Put Not Your Trust

Those who trust the powers
of knife, wand, sword,

who hold cup, mirror, globe
essential things,

who substitute the symbols
for the soul's

love-granted understanding
have begun

again the old game of a
tyrant priesthood

dignified by signs and
implements,

and cannot make of clay
the cup of Earth,

of twigs the Sword,
or of the water Wine,

or, lifting gently a
commanding hand,

give blessing from the
source of all the blessings.

Names

Do not use too many names,
for names

are separations,
and we all are one

in past and present;
names reverberate

particulars till the
unity is drowned

in vast obliquities
of sound and image;

rather speak of
Her without a name,

of Him without a name,
retaining thus

the rhythm of the breath:
Her Him, Her Him,

Her Him, Her Him, Her Him,
our endless music.

She

She is the hand
and all that is held in the hand

She is the wind
and the trembling of the leaf.

She is dance
and the quick foot of the dancer.

She is the hymn of conquest,
the sigh of the slain.

She is the explosion
of the cosmos

and the drop of dew
upon the grass.

She is the tidal
mastering every tidal

and the wave-worn
pebble on the shore.

Water Spell

When water trembles
underneath your hand

held poised above the
still and silver bowl

that you have placed in
sunlight on your table,

do not touch, but wait;
the silent message

is the one that washes
through your bones,

cleansing with all the
waters of Her will

that shawl our births
and move the moon-lit tides

and carve the land
and draw green up to light

from roots more deep
than any mind may know,

and bow your head until
the water stills

and mirrors your own eyes.
Then close your eyes.

Healing

Asked for healing,
do not turn away

afraid of failure,
or deny through doubt

that power which is yours
and is your life,

for life is
indivisible; it is

the tide that flows through
everything; we share

all that we are
and sharing is to heal

most simply–giving
water to dry land

from what is inexhaustible
in ourselves.

The Recipe

To call another to you
take a black

smooth polished stone
into the moonlight, spit

upon the stone three times
and speak the words,

envisaging that other
face before you;

this was a spell well known
in ancient Florence

as were others of squat
flickering candles,

crossed knives, bread, salt,
wine, red binding thread,

and those who cast them still
reach out their hands

through centuries to our hands
and speak the words.

Lore

When you are told to
pull the plant by moonlight,

understand that it is
not the moon

alone that brings that light;
She, too, must send it

pale and lucent,
shadowing the ground,

and She may do so
even at high noon

dazing the grass, the leaves,
the bending flowers.

On the Other Side

Once on the other side of
thinking, touch

air carefully, for it is
not your breath

you move through, but the
earth's, each turn you make

and every word a change
in life or lives;

therefore to caution add
one clear intent

that nothing may be
random or disordered

and send your mind out
on that quiet journey,

holding the vision in you.
like a flame.

The Limitation

If you have never dipped
your hand in darkness,

intent upon reclaiming
hidden power;

if you have never burned
your eyes with light

to see beyond the shuddering
skin of day;

then you have never found
that every moment

is time's every essence,
every breath

the great wind from the
farthest darkest sea,

and every word the Word
of the Beginning.

Acceptance

Accept Her. That is all
that She requires.

Tokens of homage,
sacrifices, vows,

She knows, herself a
mistress of disguise,

may merely be evasions,
even snares,

but true acceptance
needs no outward signs,

has no expression
other than the way

you trust Her equally
in love and rage,

plucking Her bloodied
fingerprints like flowers.

Checking the Claim

Should any one pretend
a special wisdom

given him and
given him alone,

do not mock until
you have uncovered

in yourself the
message of the moon

and faced illusion
in a breathless trance

that leaves you
torn and shaken as a tree

whose branches lift
above the shifting shore

enfolded in a great
wind from the sea.

Incarnation

You may feel sure
you have been here before,

but time is not a ruler;
we don't move

along it, inch by inch;
it is another

figure and has curves
we do not know.

So if you think yourself
a long-dead soldier,

sailor, slave, or even
priest, beware–

it may be where you
are about to come,

or whom you have no
further need to be,

or, some would posit,
what here, now, you are:

compact of past and
future generations

that may have been or not,
may come or not.

Light is this life
and, split, becomes a rainbow.

The Witches

When we were cursed
we versed ourselves in tidals.

When we were bound
we found ropes reached the sky.

When we were racked
we hooked our hands on mountains.

When we were burned
we learned that life is flame.

And when they said
that we were dead, we bled

into the rain that feeds us all,
and called

ourselves the future,
seeking farther, farther,

and we were born
again, again, again....

VANCOUVER ISLAND TRIPTYCH

፠

The Emissaries
for Charles Lillard

I.

The first of us on this island
was a woman
living in the forest
beside the sea,
alone except for
half completed birds,
deer without antlers,
soundless, tailless dogs,

and then from the West
the canoe of copper came,
red with the red of the sunset,
burnished, shining,
paddles dipping steadily
as a heartbeat,
rippling the copper stillness
of the sea.

Trembling, the woman
knelt on the shore, and the hornless
deer in the forest knelt,
and the wingless birds
hunched in the shivering grass
at the edge of the forest,
and the dogs crouched quaking
between the trees

as One in the shape of a man
laid his paddle down,
and, standing in the bows,
stretched out an arm
red skinned as a madrona
towards the woman,
and promised her companions.
The woman wept

and bowed her head
and saw the tears of pearl
making the shape of a child
on the red-lit sand.
Gently she laid the child
in a shell for cradle
and raised her eyes in praise.
The canoe was gone.

Tide by tide the child grew
into manhood
as the years went by
and the deer changed,
crowning their heads with antlers,
and the birds
grew wings to learn
the hurl and sweep of sky,

and the dogs found wholeness.
Then the man
lay in the grass with the woman
and she bore
the first chief,
the first people of the deer,
sending her birthcries
out into the West.

II.

We drove in from the West
through fog. The island   18 July, A.D 1774
reared before us, dark
and veiled. We were
the first, we knew, to find it.
It lay secret,
still, within its cloak
of towering trees.

We had brought a cross.
Laid on the deck,
its four great arms
proclaimed us to the grey

and cloud-sopped skies
the emissaries of James
whose ship we sailed,
whose name brought Christ to Spain

as it was bringing Him
and our Spanish Kingship
to this country,
sworn to plant the cross
in these black trees,
but the great wind arose
and swung us North
away through shredding mist

And to another island
yet the same   20 July, A.D. 1774
thick trees, dark mountains,
rocky shores. We watched
the black canoe approaching,
seven men
hunched to the paddles
and the eighth, a boy,
dancing, dancing, on the prow
and throwing
feathers out upon
the swaying wave,
giving the sea a cloak
of shining feathers,
blessing, welcoming.
We stared, in awe,
and some men touched the cross,
and then the wind
arose and mastered us
and we were gone,
leaving the feathers
drifting on the sea.

And went a day and a night
until, becalmed,   21 July, A.D. 1774
sails wet and slack,

we lay off the third island,
which was the same one
in a different place.
We counted twenty-one
of their canoes,
traded our knives, our cloths,
our shiny beads
for spoons carved out of horn
and for carved boxes,
black and white and yellow,
woven blankets,
and hats of cedar bark,
until again
the wind rose and the heavy
canvas filled;
the cross roped to the deck,
we sailed away

for eighteen days
when a fourth time the island   8 August, A.D. 1774
rose before us
different and the same.
The four arms of the cross
gleamed like dark copper
in the red of the sunset
as we swung
in towards the shore,
the sky behind us
dull and glowing copper.
Then, from land,
as we dropped anchor,
came the long canoe,
paddles dipping steadily
as a heartbeat,
and the nine men
moaning, wailing,
as if everything
they knew were lost
and all men dying
with the dying day.
We unroped the cross
and raised it up.

III.

The sun was setting and
the colour of copper

when the great canoe
with its lifted wings

creaking as if it spoke
the speech of ravens

came into the bay
from the secret West

as in memory
and beyond our memory,

Qua-utz come to judge
and to condemn.

Nine went out and praised
and mourned, nine men

wailing and keening,
nine men, each a moon

of the birthtime,
of the time to birth,

and the canoe stayed still,
upon its height,

half raised, a cross,
the four winds, the four seasons,

the four legs of the deer,
the four of death,

and the women hid
within the forest

as the sun burned copper
on the sea,

but there came no thunder,
no great wave;

no birds fell from the sky;
no shuddering deer

fell, hornless, in the brush,
and no dog stopped

short in its barking, silenced.
We grew brave,

but careful, traded
furs for knives, for cloth,

for shells, for anything
they offered, held

the judgement off
that it might go away.

IV.

It seemed a plan not made by us
but made   9 August, A.D. 1774
somewhere the wind was born
or where the tide
decided longings and rewards.
We raised
the cross and traded
in its holy shadow,
giving our knives, our cloths, our shells
for furs,
giving the fittings of brass,
the plates of pewter,
taking the skins of otter,
of mink, of bear
until the hold was dark
with the stink of dark,

then, lowering the longboat,
we hauled the cross
over to the side,
but, as if planned,
the wind rose up behind us
and the rocks
before us, and the anchor dragged,
and we
were lurching shoreward
into black destruction.
In that moment, I,
Juan Perez,
recalled it was
the Vigil of Saint Lawrence,
he that gave away
the Church's wealth
and, when commanded
to return it, brought
the folk that had received it,
saying, simply,
these are the Church's riches.
We had given
nothing. We had gained.
The holds were filled.
I named that roadstead
San Lorenzo, slipped
the anchor, called the cross
back to its bonds,
and with bowed heads
we took our God away.

V.

She that tells this story
is a woman
older than all in this forest
beside the sea;
she lives alone
except for bright winged birds
that come like children
to her beckoning hand,
and deer that rub against her

254

with their horns,
and dogs that move around her
in her ways,
and none save she
can tell us every detail
now, for other men
have come, have traded,
changing the names of things,
the names of love
and of creation,
carrying a different cross
here where the sun sinks
in a copper sea.

The Visitant
for Ron Smith

Up from the earth
a voice that is not mine
because encountering me,
and yet is mine
because possessing me,
is making words
within the quiet
underneath the moon
here in this garden
where the altered roses
nod and shudder
to the touch of wind
coming in
from the impermanent sea,
and the quiet,
like a sea-shell, holds
the hush and roar
of other tidal voices
from within or from without,
from far
dark history or
from hesitant tomorrows,
as I listen,

and the roses listen,
clenching their roots
to keep their grip on fear
and known mortality,
those guardians of
our finitude
that shield us from the light
we may not know
without undoing time;
they listen, and I listen.
I am listening.

This is your time
and my foretelling;
I am your memory
you my glimpse
of prophecy; we
are bound together
as a history
and a dance.

Can this be spoken
by a voice of mine?
Or an intruder?
I turn. And in moonlight
there beneath the yew
a creature forms
itself from darkness,
pads towards me, stares
unblinking through its mask,
its little hands
black-gloved and delicate
as those of some
frail ancient grandmother.
I stare. It stares,
then turns and goes.
I look into the dark
authority of night.
The voice propounds.

I am the racoon mask,
the mask of the bear,
the tooth of the beaver,
the silver scale of the salmon;
I am the lunge through darkness,
the leap through water,
the sudden stoop from the sky,
the final echo.
Sometimes when I remember
I foretell,
having quite forgotten
how to remember.
Am I foreseeing or recalling you?
Maybe your memory of me
is your future.

This garden is time's grave
and now the garden
is a forest
neighbouring the sea
and moss-hung,
tattered with green hanging moss,
and roped with vines
and fanged with shaking fern,
and there is someone
standing in the light
between two pillared hemlocks
and the light,
itself a pillar,
shows and hides the shape
that stands there, with
an arrow in his hand,
waits for my words.
I have to give him words.

Why do we speak to each other?
What do we know
in common? What is ours?
This land, this island,
and the pulse of

root and leaf, the surge
and suck of tide, the
moonlight and its mirror.

What about Credo,
thus and thus and thus?

Have you
seen the
leaf drop
from the
tree?

Well, then, Logic–
therefore, thus, and so... ?
Have you
seen the
tree let
go the
leaf ?

Are these my hands?
Your hands are mine.
Are these my eyes?
I see with them.
Is this my mind?
I think your thought.
You are my death.
Your birth is mine.

We are at one it seems.
I stand and know
he also stands
invisible, apart
from me and yet within.
A spreading grey
comes from the East
beyond the farthest islands
and the forest dwindles

till I stand
here in a clearing
set beside the shore
glimmering with broken
shells whose whiteness
is more radiant
than his final dawn,
and I am overcome
with thoughts of death,
the light that swallows us
yet leaves our selves
as shards to speak to others,
broken shards
as white and sleepless
as the moonlit rose
I half remember
shaking by my gate,
as once again
I question and respond,
he smiling now,
his words changed by his smile;
I feel now, at last,
his touching hand.

This is where we come
together. Here
is where you swim
in waters I have known
and touch the trees
that sprang when I was young,
and a deer stepped through
my ghost to water,
and the reeds grew through him,
and through them
the dark original stones
that made the island,
and through those the sea,
through sea the light,
and here I touch your hand.
Why do we touch?

We are together in
an ancient dream
Which is the everywhere
and everytime.
I am your son,
your father, and your earth,
your birth, your death,
your wedding to the sky,
the emptying light, the filling well,
the rose
that you will take
from moonlight to your house,
for dawn is moonlight now;
your garden stirs
around you and
the music has begun.
You have found me.
Enter now the dance.

Landmarks

I.

Discoveries recur
and are ephemeral;
they happen, startle, vanish
as a mist
lifts suddenly upon
an unknown headland,
rocks, trees, watchers,
and, as quick, descends.

I pick a pebble from the
beach; the pebble
first is miracle
and then is stone.

Discovery is the transient
only freedom:
we are released, unknown,
to the unknown,

and altered by renewal
of the first
significant astonishment
of breath:
here is an island
where no island was,
a waste of sea transformed
into a world
that could be Paradise.
Grey through the mist
it sways and blurs
rocks, trees, and, nearer,
watchers
on the shingle
underneath the trees,
and then the black canoes,
strange words, strange cries,
the unexpected friendliness
of a dream
blessed with solidities
of rope and sail
and plank and creaking spar;
this is the moment
all of us remember
and can never
quite remember;
journal entries list
the gifts exchanged,
the costumes worn, the speeches
made with hands and gutturals,
and some names,
but they do not record
that sudden vision,
the gasp of miracle
and then its loss.
I drop the pebble
on the beach; there'll be
true splendour waiting
on a different shore.

II.

Climbing up from the boat
rasped on the beach
and the heavy curve of the iron
locked on stones
into the forest,
alone in the brooding forest,
I watch in a patch of light
one thin leaf shaking
though all the leaves around it
are stiff and still,
one leaf at the very tip
of a tall plant shaking,
shaking helplessly, wildly,
as if caught
up in a private ecstasy
of music.
It stops as suddenly
as it began.

And I continue.
There are no more maps.
Can I expect a clearing,
a ruined well,
or just incessant forest?
Reindeer moss
beards overhanging boughs;
gold lichen eats
the sunlight on dead trunks;
grey lichen, stiff
as weathered lead,
snaps underneath my footstep,
and a chipmunk chatters
as a deer
leaps suddenly from brush.
I catch my breath
and think of landmarks
for my children's names.
From that knoll
there's a chance that, looking back,
I may see where I've come from

and recall
what set me climbing.
I cannot recall
more now than the impulse
to go on
however far to find
whatever place
it is that I must find,
a shaking leaf
possessed by solitary
passion, freed
(or trapped) by some
digression of the will

which, of a sudden, fails.
I stand stock-still,
confused, unable.
Wind moves through the leaves
and the whole earth has changed.
I've come too far.
Another step commits me
from my world
and to what otherness?
A rising panic
grits my teeth.
Deliberately, I turn.
There's nothing here.
And nothing comes of nothing

but perhaps the
nothingness. I face
the nothingness. My face
stares breathless back.

III.

This is what we seek
who seek the sudden
leap of the heart at a
woman's turning head,
a marble fragment

of a god, a scrawled
and fading signature,
or else an island
where no island was,
a space of sea
transformed into a country
and a prayer

as this is now transformed;
grey through the rain
it sways and blurs
rocks, trees, and, nearer, watchers
on the shingle
underneath the trees,
and then the black canoes
like drifting trees
edging towards us,
and strange cries, strange words,
the unexpected friendliness
of a dream
thrust whole into the actual
life of breath
and rope and beam and sail.
This is the moment
of discovery
uncovering time
and this they tell of,
though they never tell
that this is also every
birth and death
transfiguring the dream
and the despair
with sudden shocking unity,
the cry
of life's astonishment
at being life,
the gift of the unknown
to the unknown,
as I continue.
There are no more maps.
Can I expect
log cabins in a clearing,

and a hermit, or a crone,
or perhaps
the remnants of a well
where gold was drowned,
or just incessant forest?
Reindeer moss
shags overhanging boughs;
gold lichen spreads
itself across dead logs;
grey lichen, stiff
as beaten lead, breaks
underneath my footsteps,
and a chipmunk chatters
in a rage:
clearly the inhabitants
have left,
if ever there were inhabitants.
I blaze
a wound upon a tree,
the axe-blow echoes
back from slopes and steeps
I cannot see.
Behind me I am sure
the boat is gone.

IV.

I tell myself that these
are the nineteen seventies,
and there are no mysteries left.
A deer
leaps suddenly from brush.
I catch my breath.
Another creature glimmers
on a stump
ten paces off and then
becomes no more
than uptorn root
and tangled leaf and briar.
I wipe away the sweat
and ease my pack.

I name the landmarks
with my children's names
as I encounter them
or see them distant.
Nicholas Rock is still
a half mile off
over the other side
of the swampy meadow;
Alison river, glistening, idling,
spreads
around it before gathering
somewhere close
(for I can hear it)
to Saint Brigid's Falls.
Again I wade through tangle.
From that knoll
I should be able to look back and see
whatever ship it is
that I have left
and guess, perhaps,
the century and the cause
for which I clamber.
I cannot remember
more now than the impulse
to go on
however far, to find
what I must find.
Earth teems with musk;
I want to find a woman
wet as this wet-brown bark
whose coppery limbs
envelop me in her;
I want to fall
into the deeper sleep
that breeds the music
each leaf listens for;
I want, I want . . .
I call *haloooo, halooo,*
and time returns
as I must now return
clumsy and wearied to the shore;
my wife

has made a fire; the kids
are skipping stones
out over the bright water:
one does five.
These are the nineteen seventies.
No more mysteries.
Except the mystery of how I came
to move back in this way,
for what discovery?
And what repetition?
I repeat
myself, rephrase my phrasings,
am repeated.
Discoveries are recurrent,
happen, startle,
vanish as a sudden mist.
I pick
a pebble, clench it,
hold it in my hand.
It first is miracle
and then is stone.

V.

Halooo   Halooo

Someone no longer there
torments me with the presence
of his shade.

Halooo   Halooo

My children do not hear.
They skip the stones.
One has made ten and leaps
with pure astonishment.
If I go down
they may prove old
as if I had returned
from centuries in the land of light
or slept

their lifetimes through.
                          I hesitate.
Beyond
their dancing shapes a ship
looms through the clear
eye-dazing blue as if
the blue were mist
and there are figures on the bows
stick-black,
and gesturing. I cannot hear.
My head
bends under weights of kingship
and I shake
to hear the gutturals
clumsy in my throat
and see from all the trees around
the tribe
assembling....
                  By the fire
my wife stirs logs.
The sparks fly up and scatter
out like stars
into our history.
Is this then our history?
Or every history
reaching out to bind
us all in moment upon moment,
moments
gathered piece by piece
from all the years
of tide that have surged back
and forth upon
this timeless beach
that shudders as I call

Halooo   Halooo

The children answer back.

Haloooo
    I pick a stone.
I drop a stone.

And am returned.
From what am I returned?

There in a patch of light
is one leaf shaking
though all the leaves around
are stiff and still,
caught up in private
ecstasies of music
none but it can hear.
I hear my heart
and see myself,
a ghost upon the sands
before the ever-moving waves,
and watch
my children running through me
as if mist
or a forgotten memory,
throwing stones
again into the huge
recurring sea
as if a stone could alter
all the flow
and shape an instant
to a monument
outlasting all that we
ourselves outlast
through episodes of every
life and death
our shifting stars command.
The leaf is stilled.
I walk down to the shore.
The fire burns.

Note: In the case where a poem begins with a quotation from another author, the first line following the quotation is the line indexed.